ESTATE AGENCY

ESTATE AGENCY

Richard E Smith

Please note: References to the masculine include, where appropriate, the feminine.

Published by RICS Business Services Limited
a wholly owned subsidiary of

The Royal Institution of Chartered Surveyors
under the RICS Books imprint
Surveyor Court
Westwood Business Park
Coventry CV4 8JE
UK

ISBN 1 84219 162 4

Typeset in Great Britain by Columns Design Ltd, Reading
Printed in Great Britain by Bell & Bain, Glasgow

Contents

Contents

Preface

While chartered surveyors may not need the *breadth* of understanding of the law of their opposite numbers in the legal profession, in a number of key areas of application to property and construction they need a similar *depth* of legal knowledge.

Exactly what the key areas are depends to some extent on the nature of the particular surveyor's practice. Two obvious examples in general practice are the law of landlord and tenant and town and country planning; there are plenty of surveyors who know much more about rent reviews or compulsory purchase compensation than the average high-street lawyer.

So surveyors need law, at least insofar as it affects their own areas of practice. Further, they find themselves needing to develop their understanding of it. Changing trends or individual variations in clients' requirements mean that from time to time even the best practitioners – perhaps especially the best practitioners – see the benefits of expanding their legal knowledge. What was acquired at college or in studying for the Assessment of Professional Competence has a limited shelf life and needs to be constantly updated to maintain its currency. Even specialists working in their areas of expertise need a source of reference as an aide-memoire or as a first port of call in more detailed research.

The Case in Point series

RICS Books is committed to meeting the needs of surveying (and other) professionals and the Case in Point series typifies that commitment. It is aimed at those who need to upgrade their legal knowledge, or update it, or have access to a reliable starting-point at the outset of an inquiry.

A particular difficulty lies in the case law and above all in the burgeoning of reported decisions of the courts. The sheer scale of the law reports, both general and specialist, makes it very hard even to be aware of recent trends, let alone identify the significance of a particular decision.

The decision was taken, therefore, to focus on developments in case law and their impact upon practice. In any given matter, the practitioner will want to be directed efficiently and painlessly to the decision which bears upon the matter which he or she is dealing with, in other words to – the Case in Point.

Each book in the Case in Point series offers a wealth of legal information which is essential in its practical application to the surveyor's work. The author of each title has the level of expertise required to be selective and succinct, thus achieving a high degree of relevance without sacrificing accessibility.

The series is developing incrementally and will comprise a collection of specialist hand books which can deliver what busy practitioners need – the law on the matter they are handling, when they want it.

Estate Agency, Richard Smith

The importance of estate agency as an essential service to every sector of the property market hardly requires much explanation. However, the significance of the legal frame-work within which estate agents operate is not so self-evident. While the *Estate Agents Act* 1979 and the *Property Misdescriptions Act* 1991 govern respectively financial probity of estate agents and misstatements concerning property in the course of estate agency and property development business, only a small fraction of the work, responsibilities and indeed rights of estate agents and their clients is covered by statute. Such absolutely fundamental matters as the scope of the agent's authority, duties and responsibilities to the client and potential liability to third parties, not to mention entitlement to commission, cannot be said to be understood at all except through the case law. The challenge in this book was to provide coherent and accessible treatment of the leading cases, as well as some less well-known ones which have significant points to make. Professionals engaged in agency work will need little reminding that this is far from an abstruse academic exercise. A new court decision can actually change what is expected of an estate agent by a client. The case of *John D Wood & Co (Residential & Agricultural) v Knatchbull* (2003) is a classic case in point. It establishes that an agent can be expected to advise his/her principal of significant events or movements in the market of which he/she becomes aware. There must be many agents, and others, who would have contended for a different scope of obligation; more disturbing would be the prospect of some perhaps unaware of the implications of the decision.

Richard Smith's authorship of this book in many ways typifies the ethos of the Case in Point series. Formerly a practicing solicitor, he now teaches law on surveying courses at Sheffield Hallam University, where he is Principal Lecturer and Course Director of the M.Sc in Property Appraisal and Management. His legal expertise is much in demand at RICS CPD events, both nationally and locally. Richard's work, at undergraduate, postgraduate and practitioner levels, has required him to develop the skill of assimilating large volumes of judicial decisions and expressing the key points concisely and authoritatively. It is this skill which has enabled him to deal so successfully with the challenge presented by estate agency case law.

Anthony Lavers, 2004.
Professional Support Lawyer, White & Case, London.
Visiting Professor of Law, Oxford Brookes University, Oxford.
Consultant Editor, Case in Point Series

Introduction

The law of estate agency is almost entirely to be found in the cases. This substantial body of case law defines the powers of estate agents, their duties to principals and to third parties and their rights to remuneration. It also includes the judicial interpretation of legislation governing the conduct of agents and their duties to the client and others. This book consists of a selection of these cases, with explanatory notes, in order to explain and illustrate the law of residential and commercial agency for the benefit of the practitioner.

The law of auctions is outside the scope of this book, but as auctioneers are selling agents, some auction cases which demonstrate general legal principles applicable to estate agents have been included.

The use of the term 'estate agent'

The term 'estate agent' is somewhat misleading, as an 'agent' is usually regarded in English law as a person with authority to alter the legal relations of his principal and to enter contracts on his behalf. In this sense, an estate agent is rarely an agent at all – it is unusual for an estate agent to be authorised to enter into contracts for the client. Consequently, estate agents have been described by legal authors as mere 'distributors' or 'canvassers', and perhaps if they had been called 'realtors', as one judge suggested, some of the confusion as to the scope of their authority would have been avoided. However, estate agents do act for their clients in a capacity requiring trust and confidence, and so are subject in some respects to the fiduciary duties of agents towards their principals (*Bowstead & Reynolds on Agency, 2001*). Furthermore, there are certain acts of an estate agent that create legal rights and obligations between the client and a third party such as a purchaser. So, for example, a representation by an estate agent about the client's property may be binding on the client. In addition, the law governing commission is largely derived from cases on estate agents' commission. So it is reasonable to treat estate agents as a special category of agent alongside brokers and other types of intermediary, who are less than 'true' agents, but who come within the broad framework of agency law.

Use of the terms 'client' and 'principal'

In this book, the estate agents' employer is referred to either as the 'client' or the 'principal' depending on the context.

Whether a client is also a true principal is a matter of agency law.

List of Acts and Statutory Instruments

The following Acts and Statutory Instruments are referenced in this publication.

Settled Land Act 1882
Law of Property Act 1925
Landlord and Tenant Act 1927
Landlord and Tenant (Rent Control) Act 1949
Accommodation Agencies Act 1953
Landlord and Tenant Act 1954
Compulsory Purchase Act 1965
Misrepresentation Act 1967
Trade Descriptions Act 1968
Trade Descriptions Act 1972
Fair Trading Act 1973
Rehabilitation of Offenders Act 1974
Sex Discrimination Act 1975
Race Relations Act 1976
Rent Act 1977
Unfair Contract Terms Act 1977
Civil Liability (Contribution) Act 1978
Estate Agents Act 1979
Supply of Goods and Services Act 1982
Law of Property (Miscellaneous Provisions) Act 1989
Property Misdescriptions Act 1991
Disability Discrimination Act 1995

Restriction on Agreements (Estate Agents) Order 1970 (SI 1970/1696)
Estate Agents (Accounts) Regulations 1981 (SI 1981/1520)
Estate Agents (Provision of Information) Regulations 1991
    (SI 1991/859)
Estate Agents (Undesirable Practices) (No. 2) Order 1991 (SI 1991/1032)

Estate Agents (Undesirable Practices) (No. 2) Order 1991
  (SI 1991/1032)
Town and Country Planning (Control of Advertisement) Regulations
  1992 (SI 1992/666)
Property Misdescriptions (Specified Matters) Order 1992
  (SI 1992/2348)
Unfair Terms in Consumer Contracts Regulations 1999 (SI 1999/2083)

The text of this publication is divided into commentary and case summaries. The commentary is enclosed between grey highlighted lines for ease of reference.

Table of Cases

1
Authority of an estate agent

1.1 AUTHORITY OF ESTATE AGENT TO ACT AS AN AGENT

The authority of an agent may be conferred in the following ways.

- It may be expressly conferred by the principal's instructions or the agency agreement.
- It may be impliedly conferred:
  - by the conduct of the parties; or
  - by what is usual or customary in the business of the principal or the agent; or
  - by necessity in an emergency.
- It may be conferred retrospectively by ratification by the principal.
- It may be conferred by the principal holding out to another that the agent has authority – usually called ostensible or apparent authority.

1.1.1 Authority to buy, sell or lease

As noted above, a form of implied authority comes from what is customary in a particular trade, business, profession or place. Such authority is called 'customary' or 'usual' authority. The cases establish that an estate agent has no implied authority in this sense to enter into contracts on a client's behalf. However, an estate agent may have authority conferred expressly, or by implication from the conduct of the parties in the circumstances of the case.

Instructions such as 'find a purchaser' or 'act in or about the purchase' imply no authority to contract, but unequivocal and definite instructions to sell at a defined price have been held to do so in some cases.

Wragg v Lovatt (1948)

The Court of Appeal stated that:

> '... the making of a contract is no part of an estate agent's business, and, although, on the facts of an individual case, the person who employs him may authorise him to make a contract, such an authorisation is not lightly to be inferred from vague or ambiguous language'.

Thuman v Best (1907)

The plaintiff claimed that the defendant had, through his estate agent, entered into a binding contract to grant a lease. Mr Justice Parker said:

> 'Estate agents as such have no general authority to enter into contracts for their employers. Their business is to find offers and submit them to their employers for acceptance.'

1.1.2 Extent of authority to contract

Where an agent is authorised to contract, such authority is limited to an open contract only (that is a contract with all the terms, except the price, implied by law) and does not, of itself, authorise an estate agent to insert or agree to other terms or conditions.

Keen v Mear (1920)

Two brothers, Samuel and Walter Mear, owned a cottage. Samuel Mear instructed Thomas Cox, a land agent, to sell the cottage for £500 clear of commission. Acting on those instructions, Cox signed a contract for sale to the plaintiff, Keen. The contract contained conditions as to title.

The judge stated that the mere employment of an estate agent to dispose of a house confers no authority to make a contract, but if the agent is definitely instructed to sell at a defined price, those instructions involve authority to make a binding contract and to sign an agreement. However, that authority is limited to an open contract and did not authorise the agent to sign the particular contract in question containing a special condition as to title.

1.1.3 Authority to sign a contract

Law of Property (Miscellaneous Provisions) Act 1989

Section 2(1) of this Act provides that a contract for the disposition of an interest in land must be in writing and incorporate all the terms which the parties have expressly agreed.

Section 2(3) provides that the document or documents must be signed by or on behalf of each party to the contract.

Obviously an agent with express authority to sign a contract can do so on his principal's behalf. Is such an authority implied by an authority to buy or sell?

Rosenbaum v Belson (1900)

It was held that where an agent has authority to sell he has implied authority to sign an agreement for sale.

Application of Rosenbaum v Belson (1900)

The decision in *Rosenbaum v Belson* was made when, under section 40 of the *Law of Property Act* 1925, a signed memorandum of sale could be used as written evidence of a land contract, thus making it enforceable. So an agent's signature on a memorandum would be sufficient if he were authorised to sell or buy. Section 2 of the *Law of Property (Miscellaneous Provisions) Act* 1989 has replaced section 40, but presumably the principle in *Rosenbaum* establishes that an agent with authority to sell or buy has implied authority to sign the actual contract.

1.1.4 **Authority to receive pre-contract deposits**

A pre-contract deposit is of no legal effect (it is subject to contract) but is supposed to indicate how 'earnest' the purchaser is and whether he is still interested in the property. Since the *Estate Agents Act* 1979 and the *Estate Agents (Accounts) Regulations* 1981 now treat all deposits as client's money to be paid into a separate client account, the practice of taking pre-contract deposits has virtually ceased.

Before the decision in *Sorrell v Finch,* the Court of Appeal had held that there was implied authority for an estate agent to take a pre-contract deposit as agent for the vendor, but the House of Lords rejected this. Therefore, if an estate agent absconds with the purchaser's money, the vendor is not liable unless he has specifically authorised the agent to take such a deposit. In the absence of such authority, a pre-contract deposit must be held on behalf of the purchaser, and so must be returned to the purchaser as soon as he demands it.

Sorrell v Finch (1977)

Levy, an undischarged bankrupt, set up in business as an estate agent. He told prospective purchasers that in order to get an option on a house, they would have to pay a deposit. In this way he got several deposits on each house and then absconded with the money. Finch had innocently appointed Levy as estate agent to sell his house but gave him no specific authority to accept deposits as his agent. Six prospective purchasers, including Sorrell, paid deposits to Levy. Sorrell sued Finch for the return of the lost deposit. The House of Lords held that there is no implied authority for an estate agent to hold a pre-contract deposit as agent for the vendor and overturned earlier Court of Appeal decisions to the contrary. Whether the agent describes himself as stakeholder or agent of the vendor is immaterial; he holds the deposit on behalf of the purchaser.

Estate Agents Act 1979 and pre-contract deposits

Under the *Estate Agents Act* 1979, a pre-contract deposit is deemed to be client's money (as is a contract deposit) and, under section 13(1), when received by the agent:

(a) is held by him on trust for the person who is entitled to call for it to be paid over to him or to be paid on his direction or to have it otherwise credited to him; or

(b) if it is received by him as stakeholder, is held by him on trust for the person who may become so entitled on the occurrence of the event against which the money is held.

1.1.5 Authority to receive purchase price and contract deposits

An estate agent has no implied authority to receive the purchase money.

The fact that an estate agent has been given express authority to sell or enter a contract does not, of itself, imply authority to receive the purchase price. However, such authority may be implied by an instruction to apply the proceeds of sale in a particular way, such as to a creditor of the principal.

Payment of purchase price to estate agent

Peterson v Moloney (1951)

The plaintiff vendor employed an estate agent to find a purchaser for her house. The estate agent found a prospective purchaser, the defendant. The purchaser paid the purchase price to the agent. This money was not paid over to the vendor (the agent, who became bankrupt, appears to have misappropriated it), so the vendor sued the purchaser for the money. The purchaser claimed that the agent had authority to receive the money, alleging that he was expressly authorised by the vendor to sell the property and apply the proceeds in a particular way.

The High Court of Australia said that such authority involves or implies an authority to receive the proceeds but, on the evidence, the agent had no such authority. Therefore, as it was settled law (following English case law) that an agent employed to find a purchaser has no implied authority to receive the purchase money, the money was still due. Nor was there sufficient evidence of estoppel, holding-out or ratification. If it had been found that the vendor had executed the transfer in the knowledge that the purchaser had paid the purchase price, it could be inferred that she had ratified the receipt of money from the agent. But in the absence of such a finding, there was no evidence of ratification.

Payment of contract deposit to estate agent

Whether an agent with authority to sell or enter a contract of sale has implied authority to receive a contract deposit is unclear. However, the New Zealand courts have taken the view that an estate agent authorised to sell on terms that a deposit be paid has implied authority to receive the deposit. Whether this approach would be taken in an English court remains to be seen.

Boote v RT Shiels & Co (1978)

A vendor expressly appointed an agent in writing 'to act as my agents to sell the above property on the above terms'. In the circumstances of the case, the appointment was found to be 'well capable of authorising the agent to take whatever steps might be necessary to bring about a contract of sale of the vendor's property ...' As the contract required a deposit to be paid, the New Zealand Court of Appeal held that the agent, having authority to sell on the terms of the contract, had implied authority to receive a deposit. *Sorrell v Finch* (above) was distinguishable as relating to pre-contract deposits.

1.1.6 Authority to receive a premium

In view of what has been said about estate agents' authority generally, it might be assumed that they have no implied authority to receive a premium. However, the matter is not entirely clear. Where an estate agent has ostensible authority (see below) to conduct the full business of letting it has been held that his acceptance of an illegal premium is within the scope of his authority. Furthermore, an agent engaged to arrange the transfer of a tenancy has been held to be acting within his ostensible authority in accepting payment of a premium in excess of the amount authorised.

Navarro v Moregrand Ltd (1951)

The second defendant was an agent with ostensible authority to conduct the business of letting a flat for the first defendant landlord. The plaintiff, who was seeking a tenancy of the flat, was told by the agent that he would have to pay £225 in one pound notes. Payment of a premium for the flat was illegal under the *Landlord and Tenant (Rent Control) Act* 1949. The plaintiff paid the money and sought to recover it from the defendants. The landlord denied liability, claiming that the agent was not acting within the scope of his authority when he demanded and accepted the payment.

Lord Justice Somervell stated that as the landlord had held out the agent as 'having authority to conduct the full business of letting', the tenant was entitled to proceed on that basis.

Saleh v Robinson (1988)

The plaintiff was looking for a new flat. She was introduced to an estate agent who informed her she would have to pay £12,000 for a flat occupied by the defendant. The estate agent, who was regarded by the Court as agent for the defendant, informed the defendant that all that could be obtained for the flat was £10,000. So when the plaintiff paid over £12,000 to the agent, £2,000 'stuck in the pockets' of the agent. The defendant surrendered his tenancy to the landlord who, after some difficulty, accepted the plaintiff as tenant.

The Court of Appeal held that the payment was an illegal premium under section 119(1) of the *Rent Act* 1977 and was recoverable from the defendant under section 125. At first instance, the judge had held that only £10,000 was recoverable from the defendant. However, the Court of Appeal held that the defendant was liable for the entire £12,000 (less £200 being a valid payment for carpets and curtains) because the estate agent was acting within the scope of his authority when he accepted the £12,000. He was not simply employed to market the defendant's flat. He appeared to the plaintiff to be the ostensible agent of the defendant, apparently acting on his behalf in asking for £12,000 and arranging for the transfer of the tenancy. In these circumstances, he was acting within the scope of his authority.

[**Note:** No reference was made by the Court to the decision in *Navarro v Moregrand Ltd*, above. It should be noted that the £2,000 kept by the agent appears to have been a secret profit, recoverable by the defendant.]

Criminal liability of the principal for acceptance of premium by agent

A principal may be criminally liable for the acceptance of an illegal premium by his agent so long as the agent was acting within the scope of his actual or ostensible authority.

Barker v Levinson (1951)

An agent of a company which owned a block of flats had authority to undertake the letting of the flats. The agent employed a rent collector. He authorised the rent collector to let a particular flat to a certain person if he found that she was a satisfactory tenant. The rent collector granted the tenancy on condition that a premium was paid. The payment of a premium was contrary to section 2(1) of the *Landlord and Tenant (Rent Control) Act* 1949 and the agent was charged with an offence under the Act. It was not proven that the agent knew of or authorised the premium. The money may have been pocketed by the rent collector.

Lord Chief Justice Goddard held that the agent was not criminally liable for the act of the rent collector. The rent collector was not acting within the scope of his employment, the authority delegated to him being limited to satisfying himself that a certain person was a satisfactory tenant and then to letting the flat to her. He was not authorised or entitled to negotiate terms and was not in the position of a general agent responsible for the management of the flats. The result might have been different if he had been in such a position.

Criminal liability of principal generally

It would be dangerous to draw general conclusions about the criminal liability of principals for the criminal acts of agents from *Barker v Levinson*. Much depends on the wording of the criminal statute concerned, and whether strict liability is imposed.

1.1.7 Scope of express authority

Where the authority of an agent is expressly conferred, it does not necessarily follow that there will be certainty as to the scope of the agent's authority. The interpretation of the authority, whether in the form of a contract or written or oral instructions, will be a matter for the courts, taking account of the circumstances of the case. Normally, the courts will allow the agent a reasonable amount of discretion in acting in the best interests of the client, so long as the agent is not acting contrary to instructions. The conduct of the parties may also imply authority in addition to the authority expressly conferred.

Toor v Bassi (1999)

The defendant was the landlord of property abandoned by the tenant. The defendant employed agents to find new tenants. The plaintiff's car, which had been hired to the tenant, had been left on the premises. The plaintiff asked the defendant's agents if she could recover it. The agents refused to release it, but said they would enquire from the defendant if it could be released and added that it would be likely on proof of ownership. The agents took no further action to organise the release of the car, and the car was stolen before the plaintiff could recover it. When sued in negligence for the loss of the car, the defendant pleaded that his agents only had authority to find a new tenant, and had no authority to act in any wider capacity. They were therefore acting beyond the scope of their authority when they negligently failed to secure the release of the car.

The Court of Appeal found that the agents had a wider mandate. This was evidenced by instructions to board up the property and replace the locks and an undertaking to carry out an inventory of the furniture. The agents had also placed a notice stating that the premises had been secured against re-entry and that goods and chattels had been seized in order to be sold at auction to pay the outstanding rent, and that any enquiries were to be made to the agents. Cross-examination of the defendant also revealed that the agents were to deal with inquiries with regard to the disappearance of the tenant. On the facts, the agents had authority to deal with the enquiry about the car.

1.1.8 Apparent or ostensible authority

This arises where a person 'holds out' to another that a third party has authority to act on his behalf and, on the basis of this, the other person transacts with the third party within the scope of such 'apparent' or 'ostensible' authority. It could be, for example, that the principal has simply described another, in writing or in speech, as his agent or as having authority to deal with certain matters on his behalf. In such a case it is immaterial that the agent was expressly denied such authority by the principal. The principal is 'estopped' from denying the grant of authority. ('Estoppel' is a rule of law precluding a person from denying what he has led another person to believe to be the case and upon which that other person acted to his detriment.)

Agents must be aware that, regardless of their instructions, if the client has held them out as having authority, their acts within the scope of that ostensible authority will bind the client.

Walsh v Griffiths-Jones and Durant (1978)

A firm of estate agents advertised that they could arrange for occupation of property without the protection of the *Rent Act 1977*. Mr and Mrs Walsh, the owners of a house divided into flats, instructed the agents to arrange occupation accordingly and expressly denied them any authority to create a tenancy protected by the *Rent Act*. Mrs Walsh did, however, tell the prospective occupiers that they must deal with the agents and sent them to the agents' office telling them that the agents would attend to all the details of the agreement whereby they were to reside in the flat. The agents purported to grant a licence outside Rent Act protection, but it was held to be a tenancy within the Act. The plaintiffs claimed they were not bound by the tenancy as the agent had acted without authority.

The county court judge stated that the instructions that the agent would attend to all the details of the agreement was one of the clearest cases of holding out an agent as having full authority that he could recall. Consequently the defendant was bound by the tenancy agreement.

Authority of agent having unforeseen consequences

The case of *Walsh v Griffiths-Jones* should be distinguished from cases where the agent acts within his authority but his act has legal consequences unintended by the principal. In such cases, the principal cannot claim that the agent has gone beyond his authority – he has done what he was authorised to do. The fact that the principal did not intend the legal consequences that flowed from that authority is immaterial.

Graylaw Investments Ltd v JR Bridgford & Sons (1983)

A property company instructed a firm of estate agents to negotiate with business tenants to secure vacant possession of a building and to arrange compensation for surrender of their leases. It was wrongly believed by the company (and the agents) that such compensation agreements would not be binding in law under section 38 of the *Landlord and Tenant Act*

1954. The property company claimed a breach of authority by the agents, in that they had entered binding agreements with the tenants.

The Court of Appeal held that, although the company had not intended to grant the agents authority to enter binding agreements, they had authorised them to enter agreements which turned out to be binding. This was not the fault of the agents who had simply carried out their instructions.

Effect of ostensible authority

Every act done by an agent within the scope of his ostensible authority is binding on the principal. This is so even if the act is fraudulent in furtherance of the agent's own interest, unless the person dealing with the agent did not act in good faith, or had notice or was put on inquiry that the agent was exceeding his actual authority.

Navarro v Moregrand Ltd (1951)

A landlord's letting agent obtained an illegal premium from a prospective tenant. Lord Justice Somervell stated that as the landlord had held out the agent as 'having authority to conduct the full business of letting', the tenant was entitled to proceed on that basis. In the circumstances, the demand of an illegal premium did not amount to notice that the agent was exceeding his authority.

Lord Justice Denning agreed that the landlord was liable, but on the basis that even if the agent's acts were outside the scope of his authority they were within the course of his employment. This reasoning was criticised by the House of Lords in *Armagas Ltd v Mundogas SA* (1986). Lord Keith said of Denning's dictum that it:

> '… may have some validity in relation to torts other than those concerned with fraudulent misrepresentation, but in my opinion it has no application to torts of the latter kind, where the essence of the employer's liability is reliance by the injured party on actual or ostensible authority'.

In other words, where the agent acts dishonestly, his act does not bind the principal unless he is acting within the scope of his actual or ostensible authority. In this context, there is no difference between acting within the course of employment and acting within the scope of authority.

Conduct of the principal

It has been seen that ostensible authority arises where the principal holds out a person as having authority. Such authority may be conferred by the conduct of the principal. For example, the principal behaves as if another person is his agent, and thereby gives the appearance of the grant of authority to that person.

Townsends Carriers Ltd v Pfizer Ltd (1977)

The plaintiff and defendant companies were, respectively, landlord and tenant of premises by virtue of a seven-year lease granted in 1970. Soon after the lease was granted, the premises were used and operated by Unicliffe Ltd, an associate company of the tenant. By 1974, all rent demands were made to Unicliffe. By this time Wilkinson Transport Ltd, an associate company of the landlord company, had come on the scene. Thereafter, all rent demands and correspondence were sent to Unicliffe by Wilkinson Transport. Thus both landlord and tenant stood by and allowed matters to be dealt with entirely through associated companies, and those companies acted as if they were landlord and tenant. In 1975, Unicliffe gave notice to Wilkinson Transport exercising an option to determine. The plaintiff landlord claimed that the notice was void as it was not given by the tenant, nor was it served on the landlord. Nor did it purport to be served by or on agents, but treated the agents as the parties to the lease.

In giving judgment, Vice-Chancellor Megarry held that where a landlord and tenant have, expressly or by implication, each respectively consigned the whole conduct and management of the reversion and the tenancy to agents, then in general what is done in relation to the tenancy as between the landlord's agent and the tenant's agent, will be as validly done as if it had been done between the landlord and the tenant themselves. Furthermore, it is settled law that a landlord's notice to quit may be perfectly valid even if it is given by the agent in his own name as if he were the landlord and does not disclose any agency or purport to be given as agent for the landlord. There was no reason why this principle did not apply to receiving as well as to giving notices. Therefore the notice was valid.

Allowing the agent to carry out certain work may be 'holding-out'

By allowing a person to carry out certain work, the principal may be holding out that person as having authority to do such work and therefore be liable to the third party where that work is done fraudulently or negligently. There are limits to the principal's liability, however. If the third party did not act in good faith, or had notice of the agent's lack of authority, or was put on inquiry by the facts of the transactions, the principal may not be bound.

Lloyd v Grace Smith & Co (1912)

The managing clerk of a firm of solicitors fraudulently induced a client to transfer two properties to him. The House of Lords held that by allowing the managing clerk to deal with clients, the firm had given him ostensible authority to conduct certain types of business. Therefore the firm was liable for the fraud.

Kooragang Investments Pty Ltd v Richardson & Wrench Ltd (1982)

The defendant firm of valuers instructed their staff not to do any work for a certain client because of unpaid valuation fees. In blatant contravention of this order, an employee carried out valuations at the offices of the client. Two of these were for the plaintiffs. The valuations were typed on the defendant firm's headed paper and the employee signed in the firm's name. (He had authority to do this for the firm's clients.) The valuations were negligent, and the plaintiff brought an action against the firm.

The Judicial Committee of the Privy Council held that the employee had neither actual nor ostensible authority to undertake the valuations. The plaintiffs had no dealing with him and did not know of his existence or rely on his authority as a valuer. Although valuation was a class of act which the employee could perform on behalf of his employer, it did not follow that the employer should assume responsibility for every valuation made by the employee unconnected with the employer's business and in the sole interest of the employee. That would be introducing into the law of agency a principle equivalent to strict liability.

Failing to control or monitor the work of an employee

The *Kooragang* case should be distinguished from cases where the employer has failed to control or monitor the work of an employee. In such cases, if the employee or agent expands his activities into areas without express authority, the employer may be taken to have held him out as having authority in those areas of work.

Alliance and Leicester Building Society v Edgestop Ltd (1994)

One of the defendants, a reputable firm of surveyors, employed a certain land buyer for residential development. The land buyer was not professionally qualified. He had no actual authority to make valuations of land and buildings for a lender for mortgage purposes. He produced written valuations of hotels on the firm's headed paper. They were signed by him and appeared to be signed by a qualified valuer, but the land buyer had forged the valuer's signature. They were dishonest valuations which were part of a large conspiracy to perpetrate mortgage fraud. The plaintiff building society sued the defendants for damages for deceit in excess of £23m. The firm admitted that the valuations were fraudulent, but denied liability on the ground that the fraud committed by the land buyer was without the firm's authority and outside the course of his employment.

It was held that, although the firm was unaware that the land buyer had produced fraudulent valuations, it had held out to the plaintiffs that he had authority to value hotels by allowing him to gain and occupy a position in the firm in which, in his dealing with third parties, he was able to extend without restriction his activities as a land buyer and provide valuations for lending institutions. The firm permitted the land buyer to gain and occupy that position in consequence of its failure to monitor or curb his activities or to require him to report on his activities on a regular basis or to place more clearly defined express limits on his activities and authority.

1.1.9 Ratification

It is a principle of agency law that an unauthorised act can be ratified by the principal, subject to certain legal rules. This gives the agent's act retrospective effect. So if an estate agent's unauthorised contract is approved or adopted by the principal, the contract is ratified.

The act of an agent can only be ratified by a disclosed principal. A principal is said to be disclosed when the third party is aware that the agent is acting as an agent. If the principal is undisclosed, ratification is not possible, as the third party is unaware that there is an agency in place.

Keen v Mear (1920)

A land agent was given authority to enter a contract. Such authority only extends to the signing of an open contract, but the contract signed by the agent contained a condition as to title and so was unauthorised. Subsequently, the principal approved the contract and adopted it. It was held that in the circumstances he had ratified it and so was liable for its breach.

The principal must have knowledge of all material facts

In order for a principal to ratify a contract, he must be aware of all the material facts on which the contract is founded. The nature of the information which must be made available to the principal depends on the circumstances of the particular case. An estate agent should make the vendor aware of all facts to the knowledge of the agent which could objectively be said to have been necessary to enable the vendor to decide if he should assent to the sale.

Brennan v O'Connell (1980)

An estate agent signed a contract for sale of the defendants' (his clients) farm for £25,000 without authority. He then telephoned the defendants to inform them of what he had done, and they expressed unqualified approval. Subsequently the defendants discovered that the agent had not informed them that another person, a certain Moloney, had expressed an interest in purchasing the farm. Moloney had asked if the farm could be sold in one lot with another farm and, if so, at what price. The agent told him it could be sold in one lot at a price of £45,000, to which Moloney had responded that that was a lot of money. There was no further contact with Moloney before the ratification. The purchaser sought specific performance of the contract of sale, and the defendants contended that there was no valid ratification as they were not made aware of all material facts.

The Irish Supreme Court held that the ratification was valid. The test of materiality of the facts is an objective one. In other words, does the non-disclosure relate to circumstances which, according to ordinary business standards, could be said to be material to a decision to accept or reject a particular offer. It is, therefore, not sufficient for the principal to say that he would not have ratified if he had known of the particular facts, for his reasons may be purely personal or idiosyncratic. On the evidence, Moloney's enquiry was no more than an enquiry, and there was no reason to expect that it would lead to an offer from him for either or both farms.

Estoppel by representation

Where the principal has not ratified the contract, he may nevertheless be precluded ('estopped') by his words or conduct from denying the existence of the contract. This is similar to ostensible authority, above. Indeed, some authors claim estoppel is the basis for ostensible authority.

An estoppel by representation arises where a person has by words or conduct made to another a clear and unequivocal representation of fact, either with knowledge of its falsehood or with the intention that it should be acted upon, and the other person has acted upon such representation and thereby altered his position to his prejudice. The person making the representation is estopped from denying the facts as he represented them to be.

Spiro v Lintern (1973)

The plaintiff believed that the defendant's wife had authority to authorise an agent to enter into a contract of sale of a house. The defendant, the sole beneficial owner of the house, had not given his wife such authority (he had instructed her to put it in the hands of a firm of estate agents who supposed she was the owner) but at no time did he inform the plaintiff of this fact. Instead, he allowed the plaintiff to continue to believe he had a binding contract to buy the house by permitting him to incur the expense of employing an architect and a builder to carry out work on the house to remedy damp. The Court of Appeal held that the defendant was estopped by his negligent conduct from denying the contract of sale.

> 'Where a man is under a duty – that is, a legal duty – to disclose some fact to another and he does not do so, the other is entitled to assume the non-existence of the fact.'

[**Note:** No ratification was possible in this case as the owner of the house was an undisclosed principal.]

Worboys v Carter (1987)

The defendant was the tenant of a farm. He had fallen on hard times and was sent to jail for six months for VAT offences. Creditors were pressing, so his wife took advice from a surveyor, who advised selling the tenancy. The surveyor visited the defendant in prison to obtain authority for sale of the farm. The surveyor believed he had been given authority to sell the farm, but in fact he was merely appointed land agent to deal with landlord and tenant matters in respect of the farm. Subsequently the surveyor accepted a tender from the plaintiff. The plaintiff and his family visited the defendant and his wife three times. On the second occasion, the plaintiff pressed the defendant for a completion date because he was selling his own farm, but no date was agreed. On the third occasion, the plaintiff was allowed to measure up the property. At no time did the defendant deny that he had given authority to the surveyor to sell the farm. The plaintiff brought an action for specific performance of the contract.

The Court of Appeal were unwilling to decide the matter on the ground of ratification when it was clear that the defendant at all material times did not wish to be bound by the contract. It was held that the defendant was estopped from denying the contract. It must have been clear to the defendant that the plaintiff believed he had a binding contract. Furthermore, the defendant was aware that the plaintiff was acting on that assumption particularly with regard to the sale of his own farm.

1.2 IMPLIED AUTHORITY

There are certain functions which a residential or commercial agent has implied authority to perform. Such authority is usually derived from what is 'usual' or 'customary' in the business of the principal or in that of an estate agent.

1.2.1 Landlord and tenant notices and other matters

Valid notice may be given or received by a duly authorised agent. Such authority is usually implied where a person is given general power to manage property. The notice should state that it is given on behalf of the landlord or the tenant as appropriate. However, a notice in the agent's own name, not expressed to be given as agent, may be valid if the other party can act upon the notice safely in the knowledge that it will be binding on the principal of the giver.

Jones v Phipps (1868)

The trustees of a marriage settlement left the entire management of a farm to the life tenant of the estate, Sir Maxwell Graves. Sir Maxwell determined the tenancy of the farm by notice to quit in his own name. The tenant believed Sir Maxwell to be the legal owner of the farm. It was held that Sir Maxwell, being a general agent and not one holding a special or limited authority, was able to serve a valid notice to quit in his own name without referring to his agency. However, it was also held that the notice must be such as the tenant may act upon safely, that is, one which is in fact, and which the tenant has reason to believe to be, binding on the landlord.

[**Note:** It is helpful to note that in *Lemmerbell Ltd v Britannia LAS Direct Ltd* (below) the Court of Appeal, applying the principles in *Jones v Phipps,* agreed with counsel's propositions that circumstances in which the tenant may act upon the notice safely include cases where:

(a) the recipient knows that the giver was authorised to give the notice;
(b) the principal has held out the giver of the notice as authorised to give the notice;
(c) the recipient has been led to believe that the giver of the notice is the principal.]

Rent collectors

A mere rent collector has no authority to receive a notice to quit.

Pearse v Boulter (1860)

A rent collector employed by the landlord was given notice to quit by the tenant. The tenant then gave the key to a person who looked after the landlord's empty houses. The Court held that notice to a mere collector of rents was not sufficient. Neither was there any surrender by operation of law, as the housekeeper had no authority to receive the key.

General agents of landlords and tenants

If a landlord and tenant have, expressly or by implication, each respectively consigned the whole conduct and management of the leasehold property to agents on their behalf, then in general what is done in relation to the tenancy as between the landlord's agent and the tenant's agent will be as validly done as if it had been done between the landlord and the tenant themselves. (Vice-Chancellor Megarry in *Townsends Carriers Ltd v Pfizer Ltd*.) So a managing agent must be aware that what he does and says in relation to the tenancy may be binding on the principal.

Townsends Carriers Ltd v Pfizer Ltd (1977)

Both landlord and tenant had, by their conduct, allowed associate companies to act as their agents. Notice to exercise an option to determine the tenancy was given by the tenant's agent to the landlord's agent. In holding that the notice was valid on basic principles of agency law, Vice-Chancellor Megarry observed that it has long been settled law that an agent with general control of a landlord's property has authority to give a notice to quit, even if it is given in the agent's own name as if he were the landlord and does not disclose any agency or purport to be given as agent for the landlord (*Jones v Phipps*). He saw no reason why an agent with such authority should be denied the power to receive a notice. 'I do not think that the principle that it is more blessed to give than to receive is part of the law of landlord and tenant.'

Lemmerbell Ltd v Britannia LAS Direct Ltd (1998)

This case concerned the service of a tenant's notice to operate a break clause. The notice was served by an associate company of the tenant. The Court of Appeal distinguished the case on the facts from the *Townsends Carriers* case and found there was insufficient evidence of a general agency. Therefore the notice was void. This case illustrates the truism that each case turns on its own facts. Whether there is a general agency is a question of fact in the circumstances of the case. So, for example, the payment of and acceptance of rent does not necessarily indicate agency. It may, as in *Dun & Bradstreet Software Services (England) Ltd v Provident Mutual Life Assurance Association,* indicate a different legal relationship, such as trusteeship.

Authority of estate agents and managing agents

It seems that a mere estate agent has no usual authority to receive a notice and presumably no such authority to give notices either. However, a managing agent will normally have such authority following *Townsends Carriers Ltd v Pfizer Ltd.*

Robert Baxendale v Davstone Holdings Ltd (1982)

The tenant's solicitors served an originating application for a new tenancy, under the *Landlord and Tenant Act* 1954, on the landlord's estate agents who had been handling the negotiations for a new lease. The judge found, and it was not challenged in the Court of Appeal, that those estate agents were not duly authorised to accept service.

Peel Developments (South) Ltd v Siemens plc (1992)

A tenant's notice to determine was served on the managing agents of the landlord. The managing agents were held out as charged with the management of the property and therefore, in the view of the judge, there was a general agency. In determining the validity of the notice, he was of the opinion that a managing agent would have, among other things, general authority to receive notices relating to the property and receive them in their own name, following *Townsends Carriers Ltd v Pfizer Ltd.*

Statutory notices

Unless a statute requires personal service, the normal rules of agency apply and good service of a statutory notice can be effected by service on a duly authorised agent.

Galinski v McHugh (1989)

The defendant was the tenant of a long residential leasehold tenancy. He had failed to complete his enfranchisement within the statutory time limits and so the landlord served a notice of termination under section 4(1) of the *Landlord and Tenant Act* 1954 proposing a statutory tenancy. This gave the tenant two months to give formal notice (again) of a claim to enfranchise. The tenant did not respond within the two-month period and so the landlord claimed he had lost the right to enfranchise. The tenant claimed the section 4 notice was invalid as it had been served on his solicitors, instead of him personally. Before the notice was served, the tenant had represented to the landlord's solicitors that his solicitors were authorised to deal with matters on his behalf. The judge at first instance therefore found that he had held them out as having authority to accept the section 4 notice. This finding of ostensible authority was not challenged in the Court of Appeal. Instead, the tenant contended that service on a tenant's agent was not permitted under the *Landlord and Tenant Act* 1954. Section 23(1) of the *Landlord and Tenant Act* 1927 governs the service of notices under the 1954 Act. It expressly permits service on a landlord's agent, but makes no mention of service on a tenant's agent. Therefore the principle of statutory interpretation that the mention of one thing excludes the other was invoked by the tenant. But the Court held that the section is permissive, not prohibitive, of modes of service. It expressly offers choices of mode of service in order to assist those obliged to serve notices. The Court stated that the exclusion principle is only an aid to construction and would have expected the statute to expressly exclude service on a tenant's agent if that was the intention. The case of *Fagan v Knowsley Metropolitan Borough Council* was distinguished. That case concerned section 30(1) of the *Compulsory Purchase Act* 1965 which states that notices served by the acquiring authority shall be served personally.

1.2.2 **Authority to describe property**

It appears from the cases that an estate agent has implied authority to describe property. (Some judges have used the phrase ostensible authority in this context although that appears to be inappropriate.) Therefore, if the agent makes a false statement of fact about the property, he may render his client liable to a third party who acted upon it. Statements made by employees of agents in the course of their employment will also bind the principal. (See *Whiteman v Weston* at 2.2.6.)

Mullens v Miller (1882)

The plaintiffs employed an estate agent to find a tenant and then a purchaser of a leasehold warehouse. The estate agent made false assertions to the defendant about the value of the warehouse and the interest that others had expressed in it. In particular, he falsely stated that another person was ready to buy the property for a certain sum. The defendant paid a deposit and signed the agreement of sale, but refused to complete the purchase when the agent was unable to substantiate his claims. The plaintiffs sought specific performance claiming that the agent was merely employed to find a purchaser and that he had no authority to contract or negotiate, or to make any statement or representation, except that the plaintiffs were desirous of selling.
Vice-Chancellor Bacon said:

> 'A man employs an agent to let a house for him; that authority, in my opinion, contains also an authority to describe the property truly, to represent its actual situation, and, if he thinks fit, to represent its value. That is within the scope of the agent's authority; and when the authority is changed, and instead of being given authority to let it becomes an authority to find a purchaser, I think the authority is the same.'

Subsequently Vice-Chancellor Bacon stated that if the agent did state any falsehood on behalf of his principal which induced the purchaser to enter into a contract, this precludes the principal from obtaining specific performance.

Accordingly, specific performance was refused and the defendant's deposit was returned.

Gordon v Selico Co Ltd (1986)

Selico Co Ltd was the landlord of a block of flats. It employed a company, Select, as managing agents. Select employed a builder to carry out work to one of the flats in order to sell it. The builder deliberately covered up evidence of extensive dry rot without remedying the problem. A surveyor, the controlling shareholder of Select, supervised and inspected the work of the builder. The plaintiffs bought the flat and subsequently discovered extensive dry rot. They sued Selico in the tort of deceit.

The Court of Appeal stated that Select, through the surveyor, must have been fully aware of what the builder was doing and so was a party to the fraud. As Select had actual or ostensible authority as managing agents for Selico to sell a lease of the flat and 'make any representations with a view to selling', Selico was liable to the purchasers for its managing agent's deceit.

Gosling v Anderson (1972)

The defendant was selling a flat to the plaintiff. The plaintiff required a garage as well. The defendant's estate agent wrote to the plaintiff stating that he had been informed by the defendant that planning consent for a garage had been granted. In his judgment, Lord Denning appears to have assumed, without examining the issue, that the agent had authority to make representations about the property, and said that in order to recover damages for an innocent misrepresentation under the *Misrepresentation Act* 1967 it is sufficient that the agent made a statement which was in fact untrue, although he believed it to be true.

In his concurring judgment, Lord Justice Roskill states that the judge at first instance was wrong in stating that the agent had ostensible authority, as he had actual authority. Actual authority includes implied authority, and this, presumably, is what Lord Justice Roskill meant. If, on the other hand, he meant that an agent must have express authority to make representations, this is inconsistent with other judicial statements on this aspect of law.

Registered Holdings v Kadri (1972)

A prospective purchaser of a house was assured by a telephonist employed by the auctioneers that it was not subject to any slum clearance or other local authority orders. The purchaser bid for the property at the auction and then discovered that the house was subject to slum clearance and closing orders. It was held that the purchaser was entitled to rescind the contract of sale for misrepresentation.

No authority to make statements forming part of the contract of sale

Although an agent may have implied authority to describe a property, he has no implied authority to make contractual statements. So false descriptions of the property by the agent cannot form part of the contract without authority.

Hill v Harris (1965)

The defendant tenant instructed an estate agent to find a subtenant. The prospective subtenant was told by the agent that it would be all right to use the premises for the sale of confectionery and tobacco. In fact, this was prohibited by the head lease without the consent of the head landlord. So the subtenant was unable to run the business proposed, and sued the defendant for breach of warranty. (A warranty is a term of the contract.)

In the absence of any express or ostensible authority to enter a contractual arrangement, the claim failed. Lord Justice Diplock said:

> '... the ostensible authority of an estate agent invited to find a purchaser for premises or a lessee for premises, does not extend to entering into any contractual relationship in respect of the premises on behalf of the person instructing him. It may well be that he has

authority to make representations as to the state of the premises, but representations are a very different matter from warranty.'

[**Note:** See Chapter 3 for liability for false descriptions of property and for the distinction between misdescription and misrepresentation.]

1.2.3 Authority-denying clauses

The principal may wish to avoid liability for any statement made by the agent by denying him any authority to make representations about the property. Such denial of authority must be brought to the attention of the third party to be effective, otherwise the third party could reasonably assume that the agent has the usual authority to describe the property and that he can rely on the agent's description.

Overbrooke Estates Ltd v Glencombe Properties Ltd (1974)

Auctioneers were to sell a property belonging to the plaintiffs. The auction catalogue set out the particulars of the property and the conditions of sale which included the following statement:

> 'The Vendors do not make or give and neither the Auctioneers nor any person in the employment of the Auctioneers has any authority to make or give any representation or warranty in relation to [the property].'

The defendants claimed that in a telephone conversation before the auction, the auctioneers misrepresented the intentions of the local authority with regard to slum clearance in the area of the property. They claimed that the auctioneers had ostensible authority to make this statement, and so refused to complete the purchase.

Mr Justice Brightman held that the general condition in the auction particulars (in the possession of the defendants at the time of the telephone conversation) negated any ostensible authority that the auctioneer had.

> 'It seems to me that it must be open to a principal to draw the attention of the public to the limits which he places on the authority of his agent and that this must be so whether the agent is a person who has or has not any ostensible authority. If an agent has prima facie some ostensible authority that authority is inevitably diminished to the extent of the publicised limits that are placed on it.'

The defendants also claimed that the statement denying the auctioneer's authority was subject to section 3 of the *Misrepresentation Act* 1967. This states that a provision within an agreement excluding or restricting liability for misrepresentation is of no effect unless it is fair and reasonable. But Mr Justice Brightman stated that section 3 does not restrict the right of a principal publicly to limit the ostensible authority of his agent. He held that it only applies to a provision which would exclude or restrict liability for a misrepresentation **made by a party or his duly authorised agent**. Accordingly the plaintiffs succeeded in their claim for specific performance of the contract.

Collins v Howell-Jones (1980)

Property was put in the hands of estate agents by the defendants. The particulars of sale contained an authority-denying clause very similar to the one in the *Overbrooke* case, above.

> 'The vendor does not make or give, and neither [the agents] or any person in their employment has any authority to make or give, any representations or warranty whatever in relation to the property.'

The particulars of sale stated that detailed plans had been prepared and approved by the local planning authority for conversion of the dwelling. The estate agents provided to the plaintiff, the eventual purchaser, a copy of drawings, given to them by the vendor, which indicated that a two-storey building would be permitted at the back of the house. However, the next door neighbour had made representations to the planning department about his rights of light sufficient to have caused previous applications for permission involving the lifting of the roof of the rear portion of the building to be refused. Therefore, when the plaintiff purchased the property he was led to believe that he could build a two-storey extension when, in fact, he could only build at ground floor level. He sought a reduction in the purchase price on account of the misrepresentation by the agents and the defendant owners counterclaimed for specific performance.

Counsel for the plaintiff tried to distinguish *Overbrooke* on the ground that that concerned the exclusion of ostensible authority whereas in this case the agent had express authority to make representations.

The Court of Appeal held that it made no difference whether it was claimed that the agent had express authority or ostensible authority to make representations.

> 'In my judgment there is no warrant for the submission that where authority is direct, any different conclusion should be arrived at. The principal announces to those who are dealing with his agent what are the limits of that agent's authority.' (Lord Justice Waller)

Overbrooke clauses within the contract distinguished from Overbrooke clauses within an estate agent's particulars

It would seem that *Overbrooke* is good law as it has been approved by the Court of Appeal in *Collins v Howell-Jones* (and quoted with approval in *Cremdean v Nash*, below). However, neither of these cases is directly on the point at issue in *Overbrooke* – whether an authority-denying clause in the contract falls foul of section 3 of the *Misrepresentation Act 1967*. The clause in *Collins* was in the estate agent's particulars of sale and so would not be caught by section 3 which only applies to contractual terms that exclude liability for misrepresentation. It is therefore unfortunate that there is another High Court case where an *Overbrooke* clause in the conditions of sale at an auction was held not to be fair and reasonable and a clear attempt to avoid section 3. This case is *South Western General Property Trust Ltd v Marton* and is dealt with below. It seems that the judge's attention in that case was not drawn to the *Overbrooke* case, so an element of uncertainty lingers over the use of *Overbrooke* clauses within the contract of sale. However, an authority-denying statement in an estate agent's particulars of sale, as in the *Collins* case, is effective.

1.2.4 **Authority to delegate**

In general, an agent has no power to appoint a subagent to do any act on behalf of the principal save with the express or implied authority of that principal. There is an exception to this rule where the employment of a subagent is justified by the usage of a particular trade or business in which the agent is employed, but it appears from the cases that there is no such customary or usual authority for an estate agent to delegate duties to a subagent. The justification is said to be that an estate agent holds a position of discretion and trust in the conduct of negotiations and the handling of the client's affairs.

Maloney v Hardy and Moorshead (1970)

The defendant vendor instructed an estate agent to find a purchaser. The agent invited co-operation 'on the usual half commission basis' from other agents. One of these agents found a purchaser and took from him a pre-contract deposit of £450. This agent then decamped with the money. The purchaser sued the vendor and the main agent for the £450.

The Court of Appeal held that the main agent was liable to the purchaser as he had authorised the subagent to receive a deposit, albeit that this deposit was much greater than the usual earnest money. But the vendor was not liable as no customary or usual authority of an agent to delegate acts to a subagent had been established. Neither was there any authority implied by the conduct of the principal and the agent.

[**Note:** Note that since the decision in *Sorrell v Finch* (above) the vendor would not have been liable for the loss of the pre-contract deposit anyway, as there is no implied authority for an agent to receive a pre-contract deposit. But this has no bearing on the ruling in the *Maloney* case about the lack of authority to delegate.]

John McCann & Co v Pow (1975)

The defendant appointed the plaintiffs to act as estate agents in the sale of his flat. The plaintiffs described themselves as sole agents on their advertisements of the flat. They sent particulars of the property to another firm of estate agents but withheld the vendor's name and telephone number. The second agents copied out the particulars but put their own name to them. The purchaser found out about the flat from the second agents. As these agents did not know the name and address of the vendor, an employee telephoned the plaintiffs for this information and passed it on to the purchaser. He then went to view the property. When asked if he had come from the plaintiffs, he informed the defendant that he had not and that he had come privately. So the defendant assumed he could deal directly free of commission. When the plaintiffs discovered that the purchaser had been sent by the second agents, they claimed commission on the basis that the second agents were their subagents.

The Court of Appeal held that the defendant was not liable for the commission, as the plaintiffs had no authority to appoint a subagent. The Court stated that there is no implied authority to appoint a subagent, because an estate agent holds a position of discretion and trust. The Court rejected the submission for the plaintiff that there was only a limited form of subagency restricted to ministerial duties. Lord Denning said that '... functions and duties of an estate agent, certainly of a sole agent, require personal skill and competence.'

Ramifications of the judgment in McCann

It is unfortunate that the plaintiff agents in *McCann* put their case on the basis of a subagency. Arguably it was not necessary to do so as they could have established that they were the effective cause, particularly as the subagent merely copied out the particulars and had to refer any prospective purchasers to the main agent. (See *London Mews Co Ltd v Burney*, below, on this point.) Perhaps a better basis for the decision might have been to regard the agent as introducing the purchaser, but award damages to the client for breach of contract in setting up a subagency without authority. (It may have resulted in the client selling for less, thinking that he was not liable for agency fees.)

It is, of course, common practice for agents to distribute particulars to other agents. This, of itself, does not create a subagency and is an important marketing tool. In these circumstances it may be advisable for agents to inform prospective clients that the particulars may be distributed to other agents. Although it is not strictly necessary to have express authority merely to distribute particulars (*London Mews Co Ltd v Burney*), it may reduce the risk of a misunderstanding about the liability for commission.

1.2.5 Erection of 'For Sale' boards

Benham and Reeves v Christensen (1979)

The Court held that, in the absence of any agreement to the contrary, it was within an agent's authority to erect 'For Sale' and 'Sold By' boards.

1.3 TERMINATION OF AGENCY

General principles

In principle, termination of agency is a matter for the parties. In the absence of agreement, there is a presumption that agency is terminable at the will of either party, particularly in the case of agency for commission. Thus the principal may terminate the agency at any time before the introduction of a purchaser. However, this is subject to the terms of the agency agreement which may provide for a specific term or for a period of notice to be given.

Where the agency is for the completion of a specific task, it will terminate on the completion of the task.

Implied terms as to termination

In the case of estate agency, the courts have held that there is an implied term to the effect that if the property is sold through another agent before a buyer (or seller) is introduced, then the agency contract is automatically terminated. However, this is subject to terms in the agency agreement to the contrary.

EP Nelson & Co v Rolfe (1949)

The defendant vendor instructed various agents, including the plaintiffs, to find a buyer for her property. The terms of the agreement with the plaintiffs provided for the payment of commission in the event of the plaintiffs introducing to her a person able, ready and willing to purchase the property for £2,500. One of the other firms of estate agents introduced a prospective purchaser to whom the vendor gave an option to purchase within 24 hours. The plaintiffs then introduced a person able, ready and willing to purchase the property, but the vendor informed this person that the house was sold, that she had given an option on it, and that a deposit had been paid. Subsequently the house was sold to the person to whom the option had been granted. It was not disputed that the person the plaintiffs introduced was a person able, ready and willing to purchase. Therefore the plaintiffs were awarded commission as the property had not actually been sold at the time of the introduction.

In the course of the judgment, the Court of Appeal took the view that a term is implied that commission is not payable in the following circumstances:

- where the agent's authority is terminated before the introduction;
- where the property has been sold before the introduction;
- where the owner has entered into a binding contract to sell to another before the introduction.

None of these events had occurred in this case.

The defendant's claim that there is an implied term that no commission is due if the property had been withdrawn in fulfilment of some non-binding moral obligation was rejected. If the defendant wished to withdraw the property she could simply have telephoned the agent and told them not to send anybody round to view the house.

So in a case like this, the vendor could be liable for two commissions.

A A Dickson & Co v O'Leary (1980)

The vendor put his house in the hands of the plaintiff agents as well as other agents. The plaintiffs were to be entitled to commission if they introduced a person ready, willing and able to purchase. Negotiations ensued with two prospective purchasers – one introduced by the plaintiffs and one introduced by other agents. Eventually the person introduced by the plaintiffs signed an unconditional contract and returned it to her solicitors. On the following day these solicitors told the vendor's solicitors that they were ready to exchange. The vendor's solicitors then informed them that contracts had been exchanged with another purchaser the previous day. The plaintiffs claimed that they had introduced a person ready, willing and able to purchase as she had signed unconditional contracts.

Following the judgment in *EP Nelson & Co v Rolfe*, the Court of Appeal held that there was an implied term that commission would not be payable if the property had already been sold before the person able, ready and willing to purchase had been introduced. As this had happened before the contract was sent to the solicitors, the agency contract had terminated.

[See interpretation of commission clauses at 4.2 below.]

Appointment of sole agent

It would seem that the appointment of a sole agent terminates an existing agency as it is inconsistent with it.

Hampton & Sons Ltd v George (1939)

The client vendor had appointed an agent, Abb & Co, to sell his licensed premises. Abb & Co had introduced Mrs Shuttleworth, a prospective purchaser, but the vendor rejected her offer. The vendor then put the sale in the hands of the plaintiffs as sole agents. The plaintiffs wrote to the vendor confirming that he had agreed to leave the sale solely in their hands. They also enclosed a letter that they had written to Abb & Co informing them that the vendor desired to appoint them sole agents and asking them to take that letter as cancellation of any instructions that they had received. The vendor did not respond to the letter from the plaintiffs. Subsequently Mrs Shuttleworth resubmitted her offer through Abb & Co and the vendor accepted her offer. The plaintiffs sued for commission.

Lord Justice Du Parcq found that the correspondence, particularly the unanswered letter from the plaintiffs, created a contract under which the sale was solely in the hands of the plaintiffs. He stated that the vendor should have had no more to do with Abb & Co. The plaintiffs were awarded damages for the loss of the chance of earning commission.

[**Note:** Although not in issue, presumably Abb & Co were entitled to commission as they had introduced the purchaser before their contract was terminated and were the effective cause of the sale. See effective cause and termination at 4.3 and 4.4 below.]

2
Duties of the estate agent

2.1 DUTY TO ACT

There is uncertainty about whether an estate agent has a duty to act. Some of their Lordships in *Luxor v Cooper* (below) expressed the view that an estate agent does not have a contract of **employment** and so is not obliged to act. After all, unless he is a sole agent, his 'employer' is free to sell the property through another agent, regardless of the time and money invested by him in abortive work. Even if he is a sole agent, there is no guarantee that he will find a purchaser or the employer will go through with the sale. That is the nature of commission agency; the agent takes a business risk in the hope of substantial remuneration if a sale results. If he is not entitled to payment for anything less than introducing somebody who actually purchases the property, why should he be obliged to do anything at all? The *Luxor* approach seems to treat an estate agency contract rather like a reward or unilateral contract (Murdoch, *Law of Estate Agency*, 2003). A common example of a contract which can be unilaterally brought into existence is an option to buy land. The holder of the option need do nothing, but if he does exercise the option, a contract comes into existence. It may therefore be contended that, like the option holder, an estate agent need do nothing, but if he finds a purchaser the contract is complete.

Yet judicial decisions in more typical estate agent cases have demonstrated that in certain circumstances there is a duty to act. If it were literally true that an estate agent could remain inactive in any circumstances, then he would have no obligation to notify the client of offers received or to pass on other relevant information. But the cases of *Keppel v Wheeler, Prebble & Co v West* and *John D Wood & Co Ltd v Knatchbull* (below) establish that such obligations exist and that they arise both in contract and tort. It seems that certain steps must be taken to avoid a claim for failing to exercise reasonable care and skill (see 2.2). Furthermore, the well established duty of loyalty and trust (below at 2.3) does not sit easily with an obligation to do nothing.

A distinction may also be drawn between multiple and sole agency cases. In the latter, the courts have held that, in the absence of an express provision, there is an implied obligation on the agent to use his best endeavours, otherwise there would be no benefit to the client in agreeing to such an agency (*Mendoza v Bell*). Thus there is an enforceable, bilateral contract imposing a duty to act.

Finally there are statutory duties imposed under the *Estate Agents Act* 1979 in language which expressly refers to a contract between the client and the agent. So the dicta in *Luxor* are problematic, to say the least.

Luxor (Eastbourne) Ltd v Cooper (1941)

The appellant companies owned cinemas which they wished to sell. The appellants' auditor was acquainted with an insurance and finance broker, Cooper, and introduced him to the appellants because he was in touch with a likely purchaser. Cooper and the auditor introduced this likely purchaser to the appellants on the understanding that commission of £10,000 would be paid if a sale resulted. (The commission was to be shared 40/60 between Cooper and the auditor.) An agreement to sell subject to contract was negotiated, but the appellants decided not to go through with the sale. Having found a willing purchaser, Cooper claimed breach of an implied term that the appellants would not prevent him earning his commission without just cause (see 4.1.1.). The claim was dismissed by the House of Lords.

In reaching their decisions, two of their Lordships made statements which indicate that an agent on commission has no duty to act and a third doubted whether such an agent has to be diligent in looking for a purchaser. These statements are difficult to reconcile with certain cases (both before and after *Luxor*) and the duties under the *Estate Agents Act* 1979.

> 'Contracts by which owners of property, desiring to dispose of it, put it in the hands of agents on commission terms, are not (in default of specific provisions) contracts of employment in the ordinary meaning of those words. No obligation is imposed on the agent to do anything.' (Lord Russell of Killowen)

'The respondent was not employed by the appellants to find a purchaser. He was not employed to do anything at all, and would have committed no breach of his agreement with the appellants had he remained entirely inactive. There was no "contract of agency".' (Lord Romer)

'I doubt whether the agent is bound, generally speaking, to exercise any standard of diligence in looking for a possible purchaser. He is commonly described as "employed": but he is not "employed" in the sense in which a man is employed to paint a picture or to build a house, with the liability to pay damages for delay or want of skill.' (Viscount Simon, Lord Chancellor)

It should be borne in mind that these statements were made in distinguishing commission contracts from ordinary contracts of employment. (Lord Wright, who delivered the most comprehensive judgment on commission agreements generally, and whose observations on these matters were adopted by Viscount Simon, made no such statement.) Furthermore, Lord Romer's oft-quoted statement relates specifically to the position of Cooper, which bears little resemblance to the typical estate agent's instructions. By contrast, when commenting on estate agents' agreements in general Lord Wright says:

'A property-owner intending to sell may put his property on the books of several estate agents, *with each of whom he makes a contract* for payment of commission on a sale.' (Author's emphasis.)

This and other references provide some judicial support within the case itself for claiming there is a contract with associated duties.

Despite the statements of their Lordships in *Luxor v Cooper*, the cases in this section indicate that there is a duty to act in certain circumstances. Even if there is no duty in contract (and some judges have indicated that there is) there appears to be a duty in tort as well as statutory duties under the *Estate Agents Act* 1979. It would be a cavalier estate agent who thought he could claim the protection of *Luxor v Cooper* for simply doing nothing in any circumstances, particularly if he was engaged as a sole agent.

Prebble & Co v West (1969)

A vendor claimed that her estate agent had been negligent in informing a prospective purchaser that one of the houses she was selling was falling vacant. As this was the truth, it was held to be quite reasonable and proper for the agent to inform the purchaser so. Therefore negligence was not established. The Court of Appeal, however, examined the question of whether an estate agent owes a duty to use reasonable care when he acts.

In this case there was a written undertaking for the agent to use his best endeavours, so there was no doubt that there was a duty to take reasonable care.

In the course of his judgment, Lord Justice Edmund Davies gave an example of an agent, instructed to get a quick sale, who receives an offer but does nothing about it, not even conveying that offer to the client. He then says:

> 'According to counsel for the agents here, no liability of any kind could conceivably arise in such circumstances. The point does not, I suppose, strictly arise for determination today, but I repeat that I certainly view with reservation the submission that in no circumstances would there be any liability even where an estate agent acts and acts badly.'

Prebble & Co v West is authority for saying that when an agent acts, he must take reasonable care and that he must not do anything contrary to the interest of the client. Furthermore, in expanding on Lord Justice Edmund Davies's example, Lord Denning said that if an agent receives a good offer, it is his duty to inform the client.

As stated above, there is dicta in *Luxor v Cooper* that there is no contractual duty to act. Nevertheless, authority that the agent has contractual obligations before the purchase is completed (and the commission earned) can be found in *Keppel v Wheeler*.

Keppel v Wheeler (1926)

An estate agent found a purchaser who agreed to buy the client vendor's property subject to contract. The agent honestly believed that this fulfilled his obligations to the client. Another person informed the agent that he would pay more than the offer price. Instead of informing the client, the agent introduced this person to the prospective purchaser who agreed to resell the property to him. When the client discovered the facts, he brought an action against the agent for damages for breach of duty.

The Court of Appeal held that there had been a breach of duty, and awarded damages equal to the difference between the contract price and the undisclosed offer. Lord Justice Atkin specifically found that there had been a breach of contract by the agent. He also stated, by way of example, that if an agent failed to pass on particulars of the property, the principal 'would have a claim for breach of contract to use reasonable skill and diligence in the obtaining of a purchaser'.

Passing on material information to the client

The obligation to act in certain circumstances is a corollary of the duty to exercise reasonable care and skill (as to this duty, see below). Thus in marketing the property, an estate agent who becomes aware of any significant event in the market that might influence the client's instructions, must inform and advise the client accordingly. But this does not mean that the agent is bound to mention any scrap of information that might possibly bear on the situation.

John D Wood & Co (Residential and Agricultural) Ltd v Knatchbull (2002)

An estate agent was held liable to the client for failing to pass on information to him about the asking price of a comparable property in the same fashionable street and sharing some of the unusual characteristics of the client's property. The comparable property had a significantly higher asking price than the client's property. The judge found that any reasonable vendor would wish at least to discuss such a discrepancy with the agent.

Sole agency

The agency agreement may include an express undertaking by the agent to use his 'best endeavours' to find a purchaser. In fact this is commonly found in sole agency agreements in an attempt to ensure that consideration is provided to create a binding contract, enforceable against the client. Where it is absent, there is authority for such an undertaking to be implied.

Lord Justice Goddard said in *Mendoza v Bell*:

> 'If he employed a sole agent it seemed ... that the contract must be that the agent would do his best to find a purchaser and would be committing a breach of his contract if he did not do something, although he might not be successful. Otherwise a property owner was getting no benefit by appointing a sole agent.'

(This case has been criticised on the basis of circularity of logic by *Murdoch, Law of Estate Agency,* 2003, p. 48).

Lord Denning MR said in *John McCann & Co v Pow*:

> 'It is his duty, certainly in the case of a sole agent, to use his best endeavours to sell the property at an acceptable price to a purchaser who is satisfactory ...'

Statutory duties

Section 18 of the *Estate Agents Act* 1979 requires estate agents to provide certain information to the client before the 'contract' between the client and agent is entered into. Despite the dicta in *Luxor v Cooper*, the assumption is of a binding contract between the parties at the outset.

Likewise, Part II of the *Supply of Goods and Services Act* 1982 applies to a 'contract for the supply of a service'. Therefore, if there is no contract before the agent finds a purchaser, the duty to take reasonable care under the Act does not apply. This seems an unlikely state of affairs, particularly in view of the frequency of judicial statements as to the contractual duties of estate agents when carrying out their instructions in the reported cases on negligence and breach of duty.

2.2 DUTY OF CARE TO CLIENT/PRINCIPAL

An estate agent owes a duty to the client, at common law, to exercise reasonable care and skill. This appears to be a contractual duty, but in any case there is a parallel duty in tort.

Prebble & Co v West (1969)

Lord Denning MR said:

> 'So long as [the estate agent] has the house on his books, it is his duty to have regard to the interest of his client and not to do anything contrary to it.'

As noted above, a statutory duty of care and skill is also owed under the *Supply of Goods and Services Act* 1982.

2.2.1 Finding a purchaser

Dunton Properties Ltd v Coles Knapp & Kennedy Ltd (1959)

> 'The duty of an agent engaged ... upon the sale of a property must be in broad terms ... to do all that they can as professional men to get for their principals the best possible price ...' (Lord Evershed MR)

The defendants acted as estate agents for the plaintiffs in the sale of a farm. The farm was sold to the sitting tenant for £9,350. Three days before contracts were exchanged, the sitting tenant told the defendants that he intended to resell and asked them if they would act for him in the transaction. They agreed on the understanding that they could not act for him until the sale had taken place. Subsequently, the farm was resold for £14,400. There was no evidence of any lack of good faith, so the plaintiffs dropped their original claim of a conspiracy. However, the Court of Appeal upheld the plaintiffs' claim that if they had known of the sitting tenant's intention to resell, they might have been able to achieve a higher price. They did not realise that instead of negotiating with someone who was to remain their tenant, and therefore who might have reached the limit of his financial capacity, they were negotiating with someone who was to resell. The agents were under a duty, following the *Keppel* case, to pass on this information. But the Court stated that if there had been no loss to the plaintiff then, in the absence of dishonesty, the Court was of the opinion that there would have been no breach of duty. The Court reduced the damages from £2,000, which had been awarded below, to £250. This sum was based on the loss of a chance to get more out of the sitting tenant and took account of the fact that in any sale a right of resale is implicit, unless there are conditions to the contrary.

John D Wood & Co (Residential & Agricultural) Ltd v Knatchbull (2002)

The judge held that there is an implied term in a contract of agency, and a concurrent duty in tort, that an estate agent should exercise the skill and care of a reasonably competent member of his profession. Failing to inform the client vendor about the asking price for a comparable house, which was significantly higher than the asking price for the client's house, was a breach of duty to exercise reasonable skill and care when marketing the house. On the facts, the client had been denied an opportunity to sell the house at a higher price, and damages were awarded based on a 66 per cent chance that the house would have been sold for an extra £200,000.

Failing to inform a bidder of another, much higher, offer may not be negligent where the bidder, pretending to be blasé to keep the price down, led the agent to reasonably believe that he was not interested at that price.

Knight Frank & Rutley v Randolph (1991)

The defendant vendor refused to pay commission to the plaintiff agents, alleging that a higher price could have been obtained but for the agents' negligence or breach of contract. The essence of the claim was that the agent had not informed a Mr Potter (the eventual purchaser) of a higher offer.

In evidence it was established that Potter had said to the agent that he would 'not be budged' from his offer of £805,000 and was not interested at £900,000. He had stated that he would not increase his bid but wished to be kept informed. So when another person offered £875,000 and eventually agreed to buy for £900,000, the agent did not inform Potter of this. With hindsight the agent admitted that it was probably wrong not to inform Potter, but in the circumstances the judge found that she believed quite reasonably that Potter was not interested at that price. In the view of the judge, Potter, an astute businessman, had cleverly played a waiting game – keeping his cards close to his chest. In fact he played almost too well, as he very nearly lost the purchase and only came in at a very late stage with a bid for £925,000 resulting in the other bidder being gazumped. In any case, the judge found that £925,000 was a good price and that the defendant's hope of achieving the magic £1m was 'never on the cards'. The guide price was £900,000 and there were very few bidders in a poor market. The judge wholly acquitted the agent of negligence or breach of duty of care and stated that the litigation and the very large costs incurred should have been avoided.

2.2.2 Finding a tenant

A letting agent instructed to find a tenant must take reasonable care to ascertain the solvency of a prospective tenant. He must obtain references but need not check them unless put on inquiry (see Bradshaw v Press). It is worth noting, in passing, that many of these cases show that residential letting, an area of law fraught with difficulty, is frequently placed in the hands of untrained and inexperienced employees, with predictable results.

Cunningham v Herbert Fulford & Chorley (1958)

The defendants were employed to find a tenant for the plaintiff. The defendants obtained a reference from the prospective tenant's employer which appeared to be satisfactory. The tenant turned out to be a man of no substance or scruple who disappeared owing a good deal of rent and unpaid telephone and electricity bills. The plaintiff claimed that the defendants had been negligent in not making further enquiries when they discovered that the prospective tenant had no bank account. An enquiry with the tenant's supposed former landlord would have revealed that the landlord had never heard of him.

The judge at first instance found the defendants had taken reasonable care to find a solvent tenant, but it is obvious that the Court of Appeal were unhappy with this decision and regarded the approach of the defendants as 'a bit casual'. Lord Justice Parke stated that if the Court of Appeal were able to substitute inferences of fact for those drawn by the judge, he might well have drawn the opposite inference. However, as it could not be said that there was no evidence upon which the judge could conclude that there had been no negligence, the Court could not interfere with the judge's finding of fact. Reluctantly awarding costs to the defendants, Lord Justice Evershed hoped they would not enforce the order, noting that if they did 'it would be a still worse advertisement for them than they had already achieved'.

In passing, the Court did not demur from the judge's finding that the defendants' failure to get the tenancy agreement stamped was a breach of duty, though leading to no loss in this case.

Brutton v Alfred Savill, Curtis & Henson (1970)

The defendant agents' employee asked the prospective tenant for a cheque for the deposit and rent in advance. He replied that he had forgotten his chequebook, but would give her a cheque the next day. The employee naively accepted this offer and the tenant was given possession and the keys. The judge held that no agent acting reasonably and without negligence would allow someone in who had paid no deposit or advance rent, unless authorised to do so by the client.

Edmonds v Andrew & Ashwell (1981)

The plaintiffs were selling their café business in Leicester through the defendant agents. After exchange of contracts, but before completion, the defendants handed the keys to the purchasers. The purchasers failed to complete and eventually left the premises. In an action for damages, the plaintiffs claimed that the defendants had been negligent in handing over the keys before completion, contrary to instructions from the plaintiffs' solicitor. On the facts, the judge found no negligence or breach of contract. The plaintiffs had packed up and left the premises preparatory to moving to Norfolk for Christmas. At the time, the purchasers wanted the keys to check the condition of the stock and that the premises had been vacated. The agent reasonably believed that by handing over the keys he would be avoiding a breach of contract, and was acting in the best interests of his clients. There were perishables on the premises and the purchasers might have some complaint if the business was not run over Christmas and the New Year. Nobody at the time thought that the purchasers, reputable businessmen, would fail to complete.

In making his judgment, to which he admitted he gave 'anxious thought and consideration', the judge thought that there was a valid distinction between occupied and unoccupied dwellings on the one hand, and occupied and unoccupied commercial premises on the other.

Murray v Sturgis (1981)

Agents committed a number of breaches of duty when finding tenants for the plaintiff, including:

- failure of the accounts department to inform the employee arranging the letting that two of the prospective tenant's cheques had been dishonoured;
- being satisfied with only one telephone reference;
- not taking rent in advance;
- keeping the telephone in the plaintiff's name; and
- failing to reply to a request for a joint inspection of the property after the tenant was evicted, and thereby delaying reletting.

Faruk v Wyse (1988)

The plaintiff instructed defendant agents to arrange a company letting for his house. The agents employed an 18-year-old secretary to deal with residential lettings. The judge said that she:

> '... clearly did not have the experience, the training or the education (or ability that would enable her to acquire the training) that would fit her to deal competently (without supervision) with the letting of property. She should, quite simply, never have been allowed to deal with transactions ... from start to finish with members of the public.'

This employee took the word of a part-time barmaid who falsely claimed that the cricket club who employed her would authorise the letting and who purported to sign the tenancy agreement on behalf of the club. The agents, it was held, 'fell wilfully short of their duty' to the plaintiff.

2.2.3 Managing landlord's property

Toor v Bassi (1999)

The defendant was a landlord of premises abandoned by the tenant. A car hired to the tenant remained on the property. Despite requests by the owner of the car, the landlord's agents failed to take any steps to organise the release of the car to her. The car was stolen and the defendant, through his agents, was found liable in negligence for the loss of the car.

2.2.4 Finding information/making enquiries

When questions are asked of rating officers, planning officers and the like, the agent must take care to make the questions clear enough to elicit the necessary information. Answers to questions may indicate that further enquiries have to be made.

Computastaff Ltd v Ingledew Brown Bennison & Garrett (1983)

The plaintiff instructed an agent to find premises to let. The ground floor of certain office premises proved suitable, particularly as the agent had been informed by the landlord's agents that the rateable value was only £3,350. In fact, the true figure was £8,350. £3,350 was an old figure, deleted on the valuation list, that had applied to a part of the ground floor only. When the plaintiff's solicitor's preliminary inquiries of the landlord revealed a rateable value of £8,350, he asked the plaintiff's agent to check the figure. Instead of checking direct with the valuation office, the agent checked with the landlord's agent. A secretary employed by the landlord's agent telephoned the valuation office but confirmed the old figure, probably because she was not properly briefed and was not aware that that figure did not relate to the whole of the ground floor. The plaintiff sued his solicitors and his agents.

The judge said that the evidence suggested that although rating surveyors go to the valuation office to check personally, estate agents do not.

> 'But they do have to be careful, and they have to be careful in that they make it abundantly clear, if they are going to ask either the rating office itself or an intermediary, that the precise question to be answered is posed ...'

In the circumstances, neither of the agents (nor the solicitor) exercised the necessary degree of care, and their acts or omissions were negligent. The plaintiff company was awarded the difference between the rates paid over the term of the lease and the rates it had expected to pay.

GP & P v Bulcraig (1986)

A firm of surveyors had been instructed by the plaintiffs to find suitable office accommodation. Offices were found, and the plaintiffs took a lease. It was subsequently discovered that a planning condition restricted use of part of the ground floor to offices in connection with the printing trade. The plaintiff sued its solicitors and surveyors for failing to discover the true planning position. The judge at first instance found that it is common practice for surveyors to make an informal inquiry by telephone of the clerk on duty in the planning office. In the absence of express and more onerous instructions the duty of care does not require a search in the formal sense. However, the answer obtained may extend the duty to make further enquiries on the one hand and to alert the client or his solicitor on the other. This is a question of reasonable care and professional judgement. On the facts, there was no evidence to show that the surveyor had acted negligently when his enquiries from the rating and planning departments failed to reveal the planning restriction.

2.2.5 Valuing the client's property

Where the estate agent provides a negligent valuation, he will be liable regardless of whether there is a separate fee for the valuation or not.

Kenney v Hall, Pain & Foster (1975)

An unqualified and inexperienced property negotiator, employed by the defendant firm of estate agents, advised the plaintiff that his house was worth about £100,000. The plaintiff put the sale in the hands of the firm, and on the strength of the valuation, overreached himself in purchasing another property by way of a bridging loan before selling the house. Subsequently, the housing market crashed (in late 1973) and he was only able to sell the house for £36,000. The £100,000 was found to be a substantial overvaluation, and the firm was held liable in negligence.

The judge stated that a duty of care existed whether or not the defendants intended to charge a fee for their services, although the valuation is ordinarily treated as a part of the services rendered towards the earning of commission. It followed that the services actually rendered in this case were:

'... pursuant to a contract, which was subject to the usual implied terms contained in every contract for professional services, namely that the professional man would exercise reasonable care and skill in and about the services so rendered.'

2.2.6 Making false representations

Where an agent makes a false statement of fact about the property which induces a third party to enter into a contract with the principal, the third party may be able to rescind the contract or seek damages (see below). In such a case, the principal may seek to recover his losses from his agent for breach of duty, so long as the statement was not expressly authorised by the principal.

Whiteman v Weston (1900)

An agent's clerk informed the intending tenant, a professor of music, that he could use the premises as a music academy. In fact, as the agent knew, this would be in breach of covenants in the lease restricting use to a private dwelling house only and against causing annoyance to neighbouring tenants. After the professor took the lease, the neighbours complained about the noise. The landlord sued the professor for breach of covenant but he lost on the ground that the representation was the basis upon which the professor took the lease. The landlord had to pay both his own and the professor's legal costs. The landlord sought to recover these costs from the agent for breach of duty. It was found that the agent's clerk was acting within the ordinary scope of his employment when he made the statements to the professor. Therefore the agent was liable for the costs of the landlord's litigation.

Misrepresentation by the agent may result in the forfeiture of commission where it renders the contract with the purchaser unenforceable by the principal. This is the case even where the agent merely repeats information given to him by the client, for the agent has a duty to check information before imparting it to the purchaser.

Gregory v Fearn (1953)

The agent innocently led a purchaser to believe that property could be used for the purchaser's business purposes. When the agent sued the defendant client for his commission, the defendant was held not liable as the effect of the misrepresentation was to render the contract of sale unenforceable against the purchaser.

Peter Long & Partners v Burns (1956)

The agent plaintiff was instructed to find a purchaser for the defendant's garage business. The agent informed a prospective purchaser that the proposed local authority works would only take two to three feet in width of the petrol station. This representation was based on information supplied by the defendant. In fact the local authority's road widening scheme would result in the compulsory acquisition of virtually the whole of the property. When the purchaser discovered the truth he refused to complete the purchase and sought to rescind the contract on the ground of misrepresentation. By agreement, the purchaser was released from the contract. The agent sued for his commission.

It was held that as the contract was not enforceable against the purchaser, no commission was due. The Court of Appeal gave very short shrift to the agent's claim that the defendant could not take advantage of the agent's representation because she herself had given the information to him.

> 'That did not entitle the agent to make a representation such as he did without ascertaining what the true position was.'

He should either have made his own enquiries or told the purchaser that he did not know and advised him to make his own enquiries. In the view of Lord Justice Singleton, the representation made with such lack of knowledge as the agent had 'might well be said to have been made recklessly'.

[**Note:** For misrepresentation generally, see Chapter 3. For misleading statements under the *Property Misdescriptions Act*, see Chapter 5.]

2.3 DUTY OF LOYALTY AND FIDELITY

It is a well established principle of agency law that an agent owes a fiduciary duty to his principal as he is in a position of trust. An agent must therefore act 'with sole regard to the interests of his principal' (*Salomons v Pender*). The agent will be liable in damages for losses caused to the client arising out of the breach of duty, and a dishonest agent will forfeit his right to commission whether the client has suffered loss or not.

The common law is buttressed by provisions in the *Estate Agents Act* 1979, and regulations made under it, concerning honesty, prompt referral of offers, disclosure of personal interests and discrimination against prospective purchasers (see below).

Undisclosed conflict of interest

Salomons v Pender (1865)

The plaintiff agent found a purchaser for the vendor's property. The purchaser was a company in which the agent had a substantial shareholding and of which he became a director before contracts were exchanged. The plaintiff obtained no commission from the purchasing company, nor was there any evidence that the property had been undersold.

It was held that the plaintiff forfeited his commission because of the undisclosed interest, which was in direct opposition to the interests of the principal. In quoting from *Story on Agency*, Baron Martin said:

> '… in matters touching the agency, agents cannot act so as to bind their principals, where they have an adverse interest in themselves. This rule is founded upon the plain and obvious consideration, that the principal bargains, in the employment, for the exercise of the disinterested skill, diligence, and zeal of the agent, for his own exclusive benefit. It is a confidence necessarily reposed in the agent, that he will act with a sole regard to the interests of his principal, as far as he lawfully may; and even if impartiality could possibly be presumed on the part of an agent, where his own interests were concerned, that is not what the principal

bargains for; and in many cases, it is the very last thing which would advance his interests. The seller of an estate must be presumed to be desirous of obtaining as high a price as can fairly be obtained therefor; and the purchaser must equally be presumed to desire to buy it for as low a price as he may.'

Henry Smith & Son v Muskett (1978)

The plaintiff agent for the defendant vendors had, unknown to the vendors, agreed with a prospective purchaser, Mountjoy Investments, that in the event that the property was sold to Mountjoy, the agent would be retained by them as reletting agent and paid commission. Despite the efforts of the agent to ensure that the property was sold to Mountjoy (including the failure to pass on offers to the vendor from others) the property was sold to Sheraton Securities, who had had to approach the vendor direct.

The agent's firm failed in its attempt to obtain commission. The judge said that the mere making of the agreement with Mountjoy disentitled the agent from obtaining commission, even if it were clear that the agreement had in fact no influence on the agent's conduct of the negotiations. Furthermore, the evidence showed that the agent was not the effective cause of the sale, so this was another reason for rejecting the claim for commission.

It should be observed that the conduct of the agent in the *Henry Smith* case, in failing to pass on an offer promptly, now constitutes an undesirable practice under the *Estate Agents (Undesirable Practices) (No. 2) Order* 1991 (SI 1991/1032). Furthermore, the failure to disclose his relationship with the preferred purchaser will also fall within the Order if the preferred purchaser could be regarded as a 'connected person' as defined in the Order. Whether the discrimination against a prospective purchaser on the ground that he is not accepting 'services' is within the terms of Order is open to debate, as the definition of services is '... such as would ordinarily be made available to a prospective purchaser ...' 'Ordinarily available' has been held to mean services that estate agents would normally provide, and would not include, for example, a bribe. (See *R v Director General of Fair Trading ex parte Benhams*, below.) However, there is no doubt that discrimination is contrary to both professional and legal codes. (As to sex and race discrimination, see 5.3 below.)

Keppel v Wheeler (1927)

Failure to communicate a better offer before exchange of contracts was held by the Court of Appeal to be a breach of duty (see above, 2.2). Much of the argument in the case is about whether the agent had fulfilled his duty, having found a buyer who had agreed to buy subject to contract. So the fact that the agent had agreed to act for the buyer, in the resale of the property to the higher bidder, gets little attention in the judgments. It would not have been surprising if, in the circumstances, the Court had decided that the agent had forfeited his commission, as his undertaking to act for the buyer conflicted with his duty to the vendor. In fact, Lord Justice Atkin, while admitting that breach of a fiduciary duty would result in forfeiture of commission 'in practically every case', stated that as the agent had acted in good faith and the transaction was completed, he should get his commission. He was, however, held liable in damages for the difference between the contract price and the undisclosed offer.

Jackson v Packham Real Estate Ltd et al (1980)

This is a case heard in the Ontario High Court of Justice. (The principles of agency law are the same in jurisdictions based on English common law.)

An agent, Jackson (no relation to the plaintiff) introduced Mr and Mrs Brenzil, prospective purchasers, to the plaintiff vendor. The Brenzils entered into a contract to buy the vendor's house for $85,000. Jackson had been a partner with the Brenzils in a real estate syndicate and had worked for them before. The day after the contract was made with the vendor, the Brenzils resold the property for $100,000 through Jackson at a rate of commission of six per cent on exclusive agency terms (the usual rate for exclusive listing was five per cent). The purchaser to whom the property was resold was introduced to the Brenzils by Jackson The plaintiff sued Jackson (and the Brenzils) for damages for breach of fiduciary duty.

The judge found as fact that Jackson had encouraged the plaintiff vendor to sell property for $85,000 knowing of another purchaser who was interested in buying the property for $100,000. This enabled him to earn extra commission of $6,000. 'It is not difficult to draw the conclusion that Paul Jackson was motivated by greed', said Mr Justice Lerner. He held that it was a breach of the fiduciary relationship when Jackson failed to disclose to the plaintiff that other purchasers were likely prospects to pay more than the Brenzils's offer of $85,000. The plaintiff was awarded damages being the difference between $100,000 and $85,000 less the extra commission they would have had to pay on the higher sale price ($1,000).

A complication in the *Jackson* case is the North American practice of 'multiple-listing'. As already seen in *Maloney v Hardy and Moorshead,* in the UK a commission sharing agreement requires the express authority of the principal, otherwise it is an unauthorised subagency. In Canada, by contrast, it appears that agents have usual or customary authority to delegate agency functions. In the *Jackson* case, the plaintiff had a 'listing agent' who shared the commission with the defendant agent. But this did not alter the fiduciary relationship of that agent to the plaintiff. The judge said: 'The fact that the listing has been taken by another agent with whom the selling agent will share the commission does not alter that relationship' (i.e. the relationship with the vendor). He continued: 'The agent is required to disclose all information that he acquires which would be of advantage to the vendor.'

Acting for both sides

It follows from what was said in *Salomons v Pender* that an agent who acts for both vendor and purchaser commits a breach of duty and forfeits his commission, unless he made full disclosure and the principal assents. Furthermore, any secret commission received from the other side will be regarded as a secret profit or bribe and must be handed over to the principal.

Andrew v Ramsay & Co (1903)

The plaintiff instructed the defendant estate agents to sell his property. The defendant found a buyer. It transpired that the defendant had had dealings with the buyer before, and the buyer had paid the defendant's commission for the transaction with the plaintiff. The plaintiff sought to recover both the secret commission and the commission he had paid. The defendant paid the secret commission into Court, but claimed the right to keep the commission on sale.

Lord Chief Justice Alverstone said:

> 'A principal is entitled to have an honest agent, and it is only the honest agent who is entitled to any commission. In my opinion, if an agent directly or indirectly colludes with the other side, and so acts in opposition to the interest of his principal, he is not entitled to any commission.'

Fullwood v Hurley (1928)

The plaintiff was engaged as an agent to sell the Hunt Hotel, Leighton Buzzard. The defendant, a prospective purchaser, called at the plaintiff's office and asked for particulars of hotel businesses for sale. The plaintiff sent a letter to the defendant enclosing particulars of hotels, including the Hunt Hotel, and concluding with the words:

> 'We shall be glad to know your decision in due course, and if business is done we shall act for you at the usual brokerage.'

The defendant purchased the hotel, and the plaintiff obtained his commission from the vendor. He also sought commission from the defendant. The defendant refused to pay the commission as, at the time, the plaintiff was acting for the vendor.

The Court of Appeal held that no commission was due to the plaintiff as there was a conflict of interest. It would be inconsistent with the duty to the vendor if the agent refused to give particulars of the hotel to a prospective purchaser unless he agreed to pay commission. If two commissions are to be received, it must be on the basis that **both** principals assent with full knowledge of the facts.

Harrods Ltd v Lemon (1931)

The defendant vendor engaged Harrods as estate agents. The prospective purchaser employed a different department of Harrods to carry out a survey. The departments were in different buildings, and neither was aware that the other was acting for the other side. The survey department informed the purchaser that extensive work was required to the drains. When the defendant found out that Harrods were engaged on both sides she complained. Harrods invited her to obtain an independent survey of the drains. The defendant refused, but she completed the sale at an agreed price reduction because of the work required to the drains. The defendant refused to pay commission on sale.

The Court of Appeal held that there had been a breach of duty by Harrods, but that, knowing the facts, the defendant had elected to continue with them as agents. Therefore Harrods were entitled to their commission.

Robinson Scammell & Co v Ansell (1985)

The vendors' agent was informed by another agent that the vendors might pull out because the 'chain' above them had collapsed and they would lose their purchase. The agent tried but failed to contact the vendors by telephone in order to take instructions. The agent then telephoned the purchasers to inform them of the situation. The purchasers were rather alarmed, and asked to see alternative properties. The agent provided alternatives for the purchasers to view. Subsequently the agent managed to contact the vendors and told them what had happened and that he had informed the prospective purchaser. The vendors were surprised and upset at the agent's conduct and terminated the contract, treating the agent's action as repudiation. The vendors were able to complete the transaction because they were prepared to move into rented accommodation, and did so. The agent sued the vendors for commission.

It was held that the agents had committed a breach of duty, but were entitled to their commission because, following *Keppel v Wheeler*, they had acted honestly and in good faith and had been the effective cause of the sale. Lord Justice Purchas stated that in the case of estate agents, in respect of whom it is generally known and acknowledged that they will have a number of principals to each of whom they will owe a duty, the proposition that a conflict of any kind will disentitle the agent to commission is 'too broadly stated'.

In passing, Lord Justice Purchas also stated that 'it may well have been a breach of confidentiality to disclose information of this kind' but that it was unnecessary to decide the point in the circumstances of the case.

Multiple clients

As noted above, Lord Justice Purchas stated in *Robinson Scammell & Co v Ansell* that the duty of fidelity may be too broadly stated in the context of estate agents with multiple clients to all of whom they may owe conflicting duties. The judge was recognising the fact that in the real world, estate agents must act for many clients, including rival vendors, with conflicting interests. This realistic approach was approved by the Judicial Committee of the Privy Council in *Kelly v Cooper*, where there was a conflict between the duty to inform client A of all material matters relating to the sale, and the duty not to divulge confidential information obtained from client B. The Privy Council stated that an estate agent cannot be bound to disclose an offer to another client. Likewise, an estate agent cannot be precluded from acting for rival vendors, nor from seeking to earn commission on sale of a rival vendor's property. The scope of the fiduciary duties are to be defined by the terms of the contract of agency.

Kelly v Cooper (1992)

Agents were instructed by the plaintiff to sell a valuable piece of Bermudan real estate fronting the ocean. The agents had also been instructed, by another client, to sell the adjacent beach property. A wealthy American, Ross Perot, was shown around both properties. He offered to buy the adjacent property. He also expressed an interest in buying the plaintiff's property. Eventually Ross Perot and his family bought both properties. When the plaintiff discovered that Perot had bought both properties, he claimed that the agents should have disclosed Perot's intentions as this might well have resulted in a higher price. He claimed damages for loss of this higher price, and refused to pay the five per cent commission.

The Privy Council found that there was no breach of duty by the agents as the information was received as agent for another client. It recognised that it is an estate agent's business to act for numerous principals and that, where properties are of a similar description, there will be a conflict of interest between the principals. Yet, despite this conflict, estate agents must be free to act for several competing principals, otherwise they would be unable to perform their function. In the process of acting for each principal, estate agents will acquire information confidential to that principal.

> 'It cannot be sensibly suggested that an estate agent is contractually bound to disclose to any one of his principals information which is confidential to another of his principals.'

In stating this, the Privy Council drew a comparison with the duty of a stockbroker not to disclose inside information confidentially disclosed to the broker by a company for which he acts.

There is an implied term that the agent is entitled to keep confidential information obtained from each of his principals. And as the fiduciary relationship must be consistent with the contract, there is no breach of duty for failing to disclose such information. Neither, in the context of estate agency, can there be a term precluding the agent from acting for rival vendors, or from seeking to earn commission on the sale of a rival vendor's property. In any case, even if there had been a breach of fiduciary duty, the defendants had acted honestly and in good faith and, following *Keppel v Wheeler*, would be entitled to their commission.

It may be regarded as somewhat ironic that the confidential information in *Kelly v Cooper* would probably have been of benefit to **both** clients. However, this was not pleaded by the plaintiff (who conducted his own case) and there was no evidence from the other client or as to his attitude. Therefore it was not open to the plaintiff to allege that the other client would have agreed to disclosure of the offer. In any event, short of agreements to waive confidentiality rights in general, it is difficult to see how the agent could find out if each client would consent to revealing the fact to the other that he was selling his property to Perot.

Acting for more than one purchaser

Eric V Stansfield v South East Nursing Home (1988)

The plaintiff estate agents received information about the sale of large premises from the vendor's agents. This information was provided on the understanding that, if the plaintiffs found a purchaser, no commission would be due from the vendor or the vendor's agents. The plaintiffs approached three possible purchasers, including the defendants, requiring them to sign a two per cent commission agreement in the event of purchase, in return for disclosing details of the property for sale. All three signed the document. When the defendants completed the purchase, they refused to pay the plaintiffs' commission, alleging that the plaintiffs had not disclosed that they were also acting for two other prospective purchasers, which therefore pushed up the price and thereby the commission.

The judge accepted that it would be a breach of duty to act for more than one purchaser without the consent of both, but found, on the facts, that the plaintiffs had not acted for the others. After the defendants had made a firm bid, the plaintiffs considered themselves to be acting for them, and refused to divulge that bid when one of the other parties asked what it was. The judge stated that the duty arises, in a case such as this, when one of the parties demonstrates a real intent to buy; for example, instructing the agent to go ahead with the purchase. Even if there were a duty to disclose the possible interest of the other two parties at the outset, the plaintiffs had acted in good faith throughout, and were entitled to their commission.

[**Note:** For the statutory requirements about disclosure to the client of 'services' to purchasers, see below.]

2.3.1 Duties under the Estate Agents Act and Regulations

It should be noted that duties of disclosure and honest conduct are required by statute. The principles behind the legislation have been summarised in the *RICS Manual of Estate Agency Law and Practice* as follows:

(1) honesty and accuracy;
(2) clarity as to the terms of the agency agreement and liability for costs;
(3) openness regarding personal interests and gain;
(4) transparency in dealing;
(5) absence of discrimination;
(6) the legal obligation to tell the client about offers received; and
(7) keeping clients' money separate from one's own.

The statutory requirements relating to honesty and fidelity include, in summary:

Providing information to the client about services to purchasers provided by the agent or 'connected persons' – *Estate Agents (Provision of Information) Regulations 1991*; and information about services by the agent or a connected person requested by a purchaser – *Estate Agents (Undesirable Practices) (No. 2) Order* 1991.

Disclosure to the client that the agent, or a connected person, has or is seeking to acquire an interest in the land or in the proceeds of sale of any interest in the land – *Estate Agents (Undesirable Practices) (No. 2) Order* 1991.

Disclosure of personal interests in property to a person with whom the agent is negotiating the disposal or acquisition of that property – *Estate Agents Act* 1979, section 21. (Personal interest includes interests of associates of the agent, etc.)

Discrimination against a prospective purchaser by an estate agent on the grounds that that purchaser will not be, or is unlikely to be, accepting 'services' – *Estate Agents (Undesirable Practices) (No. 2) Order* 1991.

Duty to promptly forward accurate details of offers and not to misrepresent offers or the existence or status of any prospective purchaser – *Estate Agents (Undesirable Practices) (No. 2) Order* 1991.

Failure to comply with these duties may lead to sanctions by the Director General of Fair Trading. Further information about estate agency legislation is set out below.

2.4 DUTY TO FOLLOW INSTRUCTIONS

An agent who does not act according to his instructions, acts without authority. If the failure to follow instructions causes loss to the principal, this will usually render the agent liable to the principal for that loss.

The distinction between a failure to follow instructions and a breach of the duty of care is not always clear. For example, it would be possible to categorise the first of the two cases examined here as a case of breach of duty of care, because the plaintiff successfully claimed that his agent had negligently departed from his instructions. However, there is a distinction to be drawn between a duty of care and a duty to follow instructions. The former is about acting competently; the latter is about obedience. Even where the instructions of a principal may result in loss to the principal, the agent must carry them out, so long as they are lawful.

Papé v Westacott (1894)

A landlord instructed his agent not to part with a licence to assign the lease before he had received the arrears of rent from the tenant. The agent accepted a cheque from the tenant, payable to the agent, which covered the arrears and the agent's fee. The cheque was dishonoured. There was no evidence that it was customary in the business to accept a cheque in the context of the transfer of an interest in land. In any case, the agent had not obtained a cheque payable to his principal. For these reasons it was held that the agent had not 'pursued his authority' and was liable to the principal for the unpaid arrears.

Benham and Reeves v Christensen (1979)

Agents were asked by their client vendor not to erect a 'For Sale' board. A few days after exchange of contracts, the agents erected a 'Sold By' board.

The client telephoned the agents to express his annoyance and said that if the board was not removed immediately he would charge the agents ten per cent of their bill for advertising. The board was not removed. When the agents sent their account, the client paid it less ten per cent (£106.92). The agents brought an action to recover the £106.92 deducted from their bill.

The Court held that the agent had broken the agreement but the defendant had suffered no damage and was merely annoyed. In the absence of any agreement or variation between the parties there was no basis in law for the ten per cent deduction. Nominal damages of five pounds were awarded, so the agents were entitled to judgment for £101.92.

2.5. DUTY OF CARE TO PURCHASER/THIRD PARTY

Where an agent commits a wrongful act in the course of his employment, he is personally liable to any third party who suffers loss or damage thereby, whether the action was within the scope of his authority or not. This is because the liability is based in tort, not in contract. The agent cannot be liable to the third party in contract as the contract is with the principal. However, there is a form of quasi-contractual liability for breach of warranty of authority, below.

The rule in Hedley Byrne v Heller

Where the wrongful act is a misrepresentation within the scope of the agent's authority, the principal will be directly liable to the third party in contract. But if the misrepresentation was made without authority, or if the third party can get no satisfactory recompense from the principal because of insolvency or some other reason, the third party may wish to pursue a claim against the agent. This claim must lie in tort, as there is no contract between the agent and the third party. If the misrepresentation was dishonest, then an action lies in the tort of deceit. If the misrepresentation was negligent, then an action will lie under the rule in *Hedley Byrne & Co Ltd v Heller & Partners Ltd* (1964) so long as the requirements of the rule are satisfied. See Chapter 3.

2.6 DUTY TO DISCLOSE CERTAIN INFORMATION TO PURCHASER

No fiduciary duty is owed at common law by an agent to a third party. However, section 21 of the *Estate Agents Act* 1979 and the *Estate Agents (Undesirable Practices) (No. 2) Order* 1991 impose certain statutory duties on estate agents with regard to third parties.

In short, section 21 provides that an estate agent shall disclose, to any person with whom he is negotiating, any personal interest in the land he is negotiating to dispose of or to acquire. This includes personal interests of his employer, principal, employee, agent or any associate of his, and any associate of his employer, principal, employee or agent.

The *Estate Agents (Undesirable Practices) (No. 2) Order* 1991 includes within the definition of undesirable practices, discriminating between purchasers (see 2.3.1 above) and making misrepresentations about the existence or details of offers and about the existence or status of any prospective purchaser. So informing a prospective purchaser that another offer has been made, when it has not, is an undesirable practice. (Note, however, that an auctioneer can bid on behalf of the vendor so long as that right has been expressly reserved. An exception is made in the Order recognising this.)

2.6.1 Home Information Packs

At the time of writing, legislation for the provision of home information packs is progressing through Parliament in the Housing Bill. This will place a statutory duty on the person responsible for marketing a house for sale with vacant possession, to have a home information pack and to provide an authentic copy to a potential buyer on request. This pack will contain information and various documents concerning the property including the title, interest, terms of the sale, home condition report, and certain legal and other matters required by the eventual Act and regulations to be made under it. Only the seller or a person acting as an estate agent can be a person responsible for marketing the house, but the seller's responsibility will normally pass to the person he instructs to market the house. So the estate agent will have the duty to provide the home information pack.

2.7 BREACH OF WARRANTY OF AUTHORITY

Where an agent acts without authority, or beyond the scope of his authority, the principal will not be bound to the third party. However, by so acting the agent implies a warranty that he has the necessary authority, so it follows that the agent will be personally liable to the third party for any loss resulting from the breach of warranty of authority. Furthermore, it is immaterial whether the agent is aware of the lack of authority or not.

Collen v Wright (1857)

A land agent agreed to grant a lease to the plaintiff. He had no authority from his principal to grant a lease of the length agreed, and so the plaintiff was able to recover damages for the loss he had suffered based on the implied warranty of authority.

3
Misrepresentations, misdescriptions and negligent misstatements

As stated above, where an agent's misrepresentation in breach of duty causes loss to the principal, the agent will be liable to indemnify the principal for his loss.

Whiteman v Weston (1900)

An agent's clerk, acting within the scope of his employment, told the intending tenant that he could use the premises as a music academy. In fact this use was in breach of covenant. Neighbours complained about the noise, so the landlord brought an action against the tenant for breach of covenant. This action failed because of his agent's misrepresentation, but the landlord succeeded in recovering the costs from his agent for breach of duty.

Atkins v AD Kennedy & Co Ltd (1921)

The plaintiff's contract of sale of the lease of a hotel had been rescinded on account of misrepresentations made by his agent about the hotel business. So he had had to pay back the purchaser's deposit plus damages. He sued the agent to recover these sums, but the agent claimed to be entitled to retain the deposit as his commission.

It was held that, as the misrepresentations fatal to the sale were not authorised by the plaintiff and were made negligently, the agents had not earned their commission. Furthermore, the plaintiff was entitled to recover his legal costs in respect of his preparations to complete the abortive contract.

Authority denying statements

It must be borne in mind that a misrepresentation of an agent will not bind the principal where an *Overbrooke* clause or other authority-denying statement is brought to the attention of the purchaser at the material time (see 1.2.3 above). Whether the purchaser in such a case can bring an action in tort against the agent is covered below.

3.1 MISREPRESENTATIONS AND MISDESCRIPTIONS GENERALLY

There is an important legal distinction between a misrepresentation and a misdescription. If property is falsely described in the contract, this is a misdescription entitling the innocent party to sue for breach of contract. A substantial misdescription entitles the purchaser to rescind the contract, and this right cannot be taken away by an exclusion clause. A misrepresentation, on the other hand, is a false statement, not forming part of the contract, which induces the innocent party to enter into the contract. Therefore there is no breach of contract, and the innocent party must find an alternative basis for his claim (see below). Exclusion clauses may be effective if they are fair and reasonable. Auction particulars usually form part of the contract of sale so, if false, are misdescriptions. Sale particulars circulated by estate agents in respect of property to be sold by private treaty usually contain a statement to the effect that they do not form part of any contract of sale. Statements made in advertisements are representations. Statements made during negotiations are likely to be representations rather then terms of the contract.

3.2 FORM OF MISREPRESENTATION OR MISDESCRIPTION

A misrepresentation or misdescription may be made in many different ways. The fact that a misdescription is part of a land contract may constrain its form to matters which can be incorporated into documents, but there is no such constraint on misrepresentations. So as well as including documentary form such as photographs, pictures, plans and diagrams, they may include gestures, signs and conduct.

Mere non-disclosure is not a misrepresentation, but if a term of the contract requires the purchaser to assume a fact, there is an implied representation that the vendor is not aware it is untrue. Furthermore, if the vendor makes a representation which he subsequently discovers to be false or become false, he is under a duty to disclose the truth. Of course, a vendor cannot rely on a half truth which may be false or misleading because of what is unsaid.

Mullens v Miller (1882)

The defendant purchaser was told that the plaintiffs' property had been mortgaged for £2,000. Although true in fact, this was false and misleading in substance as it led the defendant to believe that the property was worth this amount. The security for the mortgage was not worth £2,000 and it led to litigation, concerning the validity of the mortgage, which was compromised by the plaintiffs paying off the lender and the property being reconveyed. The defendant refused to complete the purchase and the plaintiffs' action for specific performance failed because of this and other misrepresentations made to the defendant.

Gordon v Selico Co Ltd (1986)

Selico was the landlord of a block of flats. Selico's managing agent employed a builder to carry out work to one of the flats in order to sell it. With the knowledge of the managing agent, the builder deliberately covered up evidence of extensive dry rot. The concealment of the dry rot was held to be a misrepresentation.

St Marylebone Property Co Ltd v Payne (1994)

Arrows were drawn on a photograph in auction particulars to indicate the property to be auctioned. One of the arrows was in the wrong place and indicated that a substantial and imposing door belonging to the adjacent property was part of the sale property. When the purchaser discovered the mistake he claimed the return of his deposit. The conditions of sale incorporated certain 'notices', one of which stated that:

'… any arrows on photographs in the particulars are to enable prospective purchasers to locate the property and are not intended to depict the interest or the extent thereof to be disposed of'.

The judge held that this meant first, that the arrows are not inch perfect and, second, that they do not identify boundaries or interest in boundary features such as party walls. In any case, he found that the description of the property in the particulars was part of the conditions of sale which prevailed, in the case of conflict, with the 'notices'. So he held that there was a material and substantial misdescription entitling the purchaser to rescind the contract. In case there was an appeal on this point, the judge also held that the position of the arrows amounted to a misrepresentation and that clauses in the contract which purported to exclude liability for errors were not fair and reasonable in the circumstances of the case.

[**Note:** See below at 3.7 as to the requirement of reasonableness in exclusion clauses.]

Atlantic Estates Ltd v Ezekiel (1991)

The plaintiff landlords put a property up for auction. Particulars in the auction catalogue described the trade of the property as a wine bar and included a photograph which showed what appeared to be a wine bar in use, with customers entering or leaving the premises. In fact, the tenant had lost his licence and the premises were not currently used as a wine bar.

The defendant attended the auction and, relying solely on the auction catalogue, purchased the property. When he discovered that the tenant had lost his licence and was in rent arrears, he refused to complete the contract. The plaintiffs sought an order of specific performance which was granted by the court of first instance, so the defendant appealed.

The Court of Appeal found that, taken together, the words and the photograph amounted to more than a representation that the wine bar was the permitted user, but that there was an existing on-licence. This amounted to a misrepresentation which justified the purchaser in refusing to complete the purchase.

[**Note:** See *Lewin v Barratt Homes Ltd*, below, for a case under the Property Misdescriptions Act concerning a misleading illustration.]

3.3 STATEMENTS OF FACT AND OTHER TYPES OF STATEMENT

A misrepresentation is a false statement of fact. A statement of opinion, honestly held, is not a statement of fact, for it is not falsifiable. However, if the facts behind the opinion provide no reasonable justification for holding it, it will be held to be a misrepresentation. If the opinion is not held, there is a false statement of fact about the state of mind of the person making the statement.

Similarly, a promise is not a statement of fact, so if it is broken it is not a misrepresentation, so long as the promise was genuine. (There may be other remedies if it is a contractual promise.) If the maker of the promise did not intend to keep the promise, there would be a misrepresentation as to his intention – a false statement of fact.

Smith v Land and House Property Corporation (1884)

A hotel was described in auction particulars as being 'let to Mr Frederick Fleck (a most desirable tenant) … thus offering a first-class investment'. In fact Mr Fleck had only paid the Lady Day rent in driblets under pressure and had not paid the Midsummer rent at the time of the auction. He subsequently went into liquidation. It was held that the description 'a most desirable tenant' was not a mere expression of opinion. It was a false assertion that nothing had occurred which indicated that the tenant was undesirable.

Lewin v Barratt Homes Ltd (2000)

Purchasers were shown pictures by the defendant house builder of a house type which was being offered for sale. In fact, the defendant knew that, for planning reasons, it could not build houses of this type. It was contended for the defendant that the information amounted to promises as to the future and not statements of existing fact. The Court held that by showing pictures of a particular design of house, the defendant was stating that was how it proposed to build the houses. That was a false statement of present intention.

Mere puffs

Puffing is salesman's talk eulogising the good points of a property or article for sale, such as 'exceptional house' or 'outstanding property', and resembles the distinction between opinion and fact. It is important that the puffing or exaggerating is confined within reasonable limits. If the 'puff' appears to be supported by facts and figures (such as earning capacity of a property) it may well be a misrepresentation.

Registered Holdings v Kadri (1971)

A house was put up for sale by auction. It was in a slum clearance area subject to a provisional compulsory purchase order and part of the house was subject to a closing order because it was unfit for human habitation. This part included the kitchen and the lavatory. The vendors were aware of the orders but did not inform the auctioneer. At the auction, when the bidding was slack, the auctioneer described the property as a 'nice house' in order to encourage bidding. Mr Justice Goff stated that by no stretch of the imagination could a house subject to slum clearance and closing orders be described as 'nice'. He held that the description went beyond the realm of puff and was a misrepresentation. The contract of sale was rescinded.

3.4 REMEDIES AGAINST THE PRINCIPAL FOR AGENT'S MISREPRESENTATION

A misrepresentation, not being a term of the contract, does not give rise to an action for breach of contract at common law, but if the misrepresentation is fraudulent, the innocent party can obtain rescission and sue for damages in the tort of deceit. However, the remedies for non-fraudulent misrepresentation were inadequate until the *Misrepresentation Act* 1967 became law, below. So, where fraud could not be established, injured parties made desperate attempts to try to prove that the misrepresentation had become a term of the contract or a 'collateral warranty'. Where the statement had been made by an agent, this would be difficult to establish, as an agent has no implied authority to make a contractual term or collateral warranty. The plaintiff would have to demonstrate that the agent had the necessary authority.

Hill v Harris (1965)

A misrepresentation by an agent was said by the Court not to amount to a contractual term.

> 'It may well be that he has authority to make representations as to the state of the premises, but representations are a very different matter from warranty' (Lord Justice Diplock)

3.5   FRAUDULENT MISREPRESENTATION OF THE AGENT – TORT OF DECEIT

Where a managing agent, exercising his usual authority, makes a fraudulent misrepresentation about the property, his principal will be liable in the tort of deceit. The agent is personally liable also, as the liability is in tort, not contract.

Gordon v Selico Co Ltd (1986)

A builder concealed dry rot. The managing agent was a party to this deceit and so was held liable in tort to the purchaser.

Where an agent is authorised by the principal to make a particular statement which the principal knows to be false but the agent believes to be true, the principal is liable in deceit and cannot hide behind the agent's innocence. (But agents should check such information before repeating it – *Peter Long & Partners v Burns*, above). However, if the principal gave no such authority and is unaware of the misrepresentation, it is not fraudulent.

Armstrong v Strain (1952)

The defendant owned a bungalow in Southend which had been underpinned five times because of shrinkage of the clay soil on which it stood. On the last occasion, the property was also substantially redecorated and then put up for sale. The defendant engaged a firm of estate agents, but did not inform them of the underpinning. One of the partners of the firm told the plaintiff that he had seen the bungalow and that any building society would lend £1,200 on it. Another agent told him that it was a very nice house. Both these statements were found to have been honestly made. The evidence did not show that the defendant had any knowledge of what the agents said. Neither had he given the agent any authority to make such statements.

Soon after the plaintiffs moved in, cracks appeared because the bungalow was settling further. The Court heard evidence to the effect that a reputable estate agent, knowing the history of the building, would have advised a building society to have nothing to do with it and sent no applicant to see it.

The plaintiffs alleged that as the principal knew the truth and there was no division between principal and agent, there was a fraudulent misrepresentation. The Court of Appeal held that there was no fraud as neither principal or agent had acted dishonestly.

Some observations on Armstrong v Strain

It does not follow from the case of *Armstrong v Strain* that a company cannot be liable if one of its servants makes an innocent misrepresentation which another would know to be false. Knowledge of the servants and employees is knowledge of the company.

Armstrong v Strain is of less significance to innocent purchasers today because damages for non-fraudulent misrepresentation may be sought under the *Misrepresentation Act* 1967. But as far as the defendant is concerned, avoiding the taint of fraud is still of great significance, not least because of the possibility of criminal proceedings.

3.6 NON-FRAUDULENT MISREPRESENTATION OF THE AGENT

Before the *Misrepresentation Act* 1967 became law, a third party's remedies for a non-fraudulent misrepresentation were somewhat limited. He could, in appropriate cases, seek the equitable remedy of rescission; a rather drastic solution to what could be a relatively minor defect. Furthermore, rescission could not be obtained where the sale was completed even if the parties could be put back in their pre-contractual positions. He could also defend an action for specific performance when refusing to complete a purchase, as in *Mullens v Miller* (above), or defend an action for breach of covenant in a lease.

3.6.1 Misrepresentation Act 1967

It was recognised that the remedies for misrepresentation were inadequate, so the *Misrepresentation Act* 1967 was passed following certain recommendations of the Law Commission.

Section 1 allows rescission to be sought for a non-fraudulent misrepresentation even after the contract has been performed (such as completion of the purchase) or where the misrepresentation has become a term of the contract. Section 2 makes damages available for non-fraudulent misrepresentation in certain circumstances.

Negligent misrepresentation – section 2(1)

The effect of this subsection is that where the person who made a false representation honestly believed the representation to be true, he will be liable in damages for loss caused, unless he proves that he had reasonable ground to believe that the facts represented were true.

Thus the principal will be liable in damages for the agent's negligent misrepresentation. The burden of proving reasonable grounds is upon the principal.

Innocent misrepresentation – section 2(2)

Where the person making the representation was not fraudulent, section 2(2) provides that if the Court could have rescinded the contract, they can now award damages instead if it would be equitable to do so. The effect of this is that the victim of an innocent misrepresentation (a representation made without fault) may be awarded damages instead of rescission at the Court's discretion. So the principal may have to pay damages where the contract is not rescinded. (If the misrepresentation was negligent, the injured party can seek damages instead of or as well as rescinding.)

It remains the case that if an agent makes a misrepresentation within his authority, and a third party relies on it, the agent will be liable to his principal for the ensuing loss. He may also forfeit his commission as the sale may not be enforceable (*Peter Long & Partners v Burns*).

3.7 EXCLUDING LIABILITY FOR MISREPRESENTATIONS

Any attempt to exclude liability for misrepresentation is subject to section 3 of the *Misrepresentation Act* 1967. In effect this means that the exclusion clause must be reasonable. Section 3 provides:

> 'If a contract contains a term which would exclude or restrict–
>
> (a) any liability to which a party to a contract may be subject by reason of any misrepresentation made by him before the contract was made; or
> (b) any remedy available to another party to the contract by reason of such a misrepresentation,
>
> that term shall be of no effect except in so far as it satisfies the requirement of reasonableness as stated in section 11(1) of the *Unfair Contract Terms Act* 1977; and

it is for those claiming that the term satisfies that requirement to show that it does.'

Section 11(1) of the *Unfair Contract Terms Act* 1977 provides:

'In relation to a contract term, the requirement of reasonableness for the purposes of this Part of this Act [and] section 3 of the Misrepresentation Act 1967 ... is that the term shall have been a fair and reasonable one to be included having regard to the circumstances which were, or ought reasonably to have been, known to or in the contemplation of the parties when the contract was made.'

As stated above, section 3 of the *Misrepresentation Act* has no application to an authority-denying statement, according to Mr Justice Brightman in *Overbrooke Estates Ltd v Glencombe Properties Ltd.* But see *South Western General Property Trust v Marton* below, where a different conclusion was reached.

Cremdean Properties Ltd v Nash (1977)

In an invitation to tender, published by the defendants' agents, premises for sale were described as being with the benefit of planning consent for approximately 17,900 square feet of offices.

After purchasing the premises, the plaintiffs discovered that only 14,700 square feet was available. The plaintiffs sought rescission of the contract. The defendants claimed the benefit of an exclusion clause in a footnote to the conditions of sale. This stated that the particulars were only for the convenience of an intending purchaser, their accuracy was not guaranteed, any error, omission or misdescription shall not annul the sale or be grounds on which compensation may be claimed, and the purchaser must rely on his own inspection. The defendants claimed that section 3 did not apply to this exclusion clause and relied, in part, on the judgment in the *Overbrooke* case.

Whilst agreeing with the judgment in *Overbrooke*, the Court of Appeal held that it had no bearing on the case. This was not a case of an authority-denying statement. The description in the particulars was a misrepresentation and therefore subject to section 3. Section 3 cannot be avoided by claiming that a description is not a representation and should not be relied upon.

St Marylebone Property Co Ltd v Payne (1994)

Arrows were drawn on a photograph in auction particulars to indicate the property to be auctioned. One of the arrows was in the wrong place and indicated that adjacent property was part of the sale property. When the purchaser discovered the mistake he claimed the return of his deposit. Various exclusion clauses put the burden on the purchaser to verify information independently and denied any remedy for any error.

The judge held that the clauses were not fair and reasonable in the context of auction particulars 'dominated by a colour photograph which was completely misleading as to the extent of the property being sold' and on which it was fully to be expected that an investment purchaser would rely. So the exclusion clauses fell foul of section 3 of the *Misrepresentation Act* 1967.

South Western General Property Co Ltd v Marton (1982)

Land owned by the plaintiff was sold by auction to the defendant. The land was described in the auction catalogue as 'long leasehold building land'. The catalogue also stated that planning consent had been refused in 1972 because the proposed house was out of character with the existing development. What the catalogue did not say was that the refusal of consent was upheld on appeal and that the inspector had based his decision on an additional ground – that the house would be infill development detrimental to the visual amenities of the occupiers of nearby residential properties. This reason had been taken up by the planning authority as justification for refusal of planning permission for a subsequent application in 1981 and again in 1982. After the defendant purchased the property he sought to rescind the contract on the ground of innocent misrepresentation. The plaintiff brought an action for damages on the resale of the land at £4,400 less than the defendant had bid. The principal question for the judge was whether the conditions of sale were fair and reasonable under section 3 of the *Misrepresentation Act* 1967 and section 11 of the *Unfair Contract Terms Act* 1977. The conditions were those commonly found in sale contracts and included:

> '... any incorrect statement or error or omission ... shall not annul the sale ...'

> '... the purchaser shall take the properties as they are under the said [planning] Acts ...'

> '... all statements are made without responsibility on the part of the auctioneers or the vendor ... and any intending purchaser must satisfy himself by inspection or otherwise as to the correctness of each statement contained in the particulars ...'

> '... the vendor does not make or give any representation or warranty in relation to the property nor has the auctioneer or any person in the employment of the auctioneers any authority to do so on his behalf.'

In the circumstances, the judge held that it was not fair and reasonable to include these conditions of sale. He noted that the planning history of the land was something peculiarly within the knowledge of the plaintiffs, as they had owned the land since 1977 and had lost the planning appeal. He also observed that the very nature of the sale was to sell the land as building land and the attitude of the local planning authority was some indication that the land was not likely to be building land at all.

Conflict with *Overbrooke v Glencombe*

It is important to note that the fourth condition, set out above in the *South Western General* case, is a clause denying the auctioneer authority to describe the property. It has been seen that in the *Overbrooke* case, such an authority-denying clause in the contract was held not to be subject to section 3 of the *Misrepresentation Act* 1967. It seems that the decision in *Overbrooke* was not brought to the judge's attention in *South Western General*, and he treated the clause simply as a way of avoiding the Act. It follows that on this particular point

Overbrooke appears to be the law, especially as it has been approved in two Court of Appeal decisions, *Collins v Howell-Jones* and *Cremdean v Nash*. But neither of those decisions is on the point directly at issue and so are not binding. The *Collins* case was about an *Overbrooke* type clause in an estate agent's particulars of sale, not within the contract of sale, and *Cremdean v Nash* concerned a different sort of clause altogether. Therefore it may be open to another court to come to the view that section 3 does apply to *Overbrooke* clauses that form part of the contract of sale.

3.8 NEGLIGENT MISSTATEMENTS UNDER THE RULE IN HEDLEY BYRNE

Where the agent makes a misrepresentation within the scope of his authority, the principal will be liable to the third party in contract. But if the misrepresentation was made without authority, or if the third party can get no satisfactory recompense from the principal because of insolvency or some other reason, or if there was no contract, the third party may wish to pursue a claim against the agent. This claim must lie in tort, as there is no contract between the agent and the third party. If the misrepresentation was dishonest, then an action lies in the tort of deceit (see 3.5 above). If the misrepresentation was negligent, then an action may lie under the rule in *Hedley Byrne & Co Ltd v Heller & Partners Ltd*. In determining the application of the rule, the courts apply the triple test of foreseeability, proximity and whether it is fair, just and reasonable that the law should impose a duty of a given scope upon the one party for the benefit of the other. In essence, the necessary relationship of proximity between the maker of a statement and the person who relies upon it exists where:

(1) advice is required for a purpose known to the adviser when the advice is given;

(2) the adviser knows that the advice will be communicated to the advisee; in order to be used for that purpose;

(3) it is known that the advice is likely to be acted upon by the advisee for that purpose without independent inquiry;

(4) it is so acted upon by the advisee to his detriment.

(Lord Oliver in *Caparo Industries plc v Dickman*)

The application of these rules has resulted in agents being personally liable to third parties for negligent misstatements. Agents must also be aware that the rule in *Hedley Byrne* does not just apply to statements of fact, but also to statements of professional opinion or advice upon which the third party relies. In this respect, negligent misstatements are wider than a contractual misrepresentation in the specific sense, above, of a false statement of fact inducing a party to enter into a contract.

Principals should be aware that, even though they may have no contract with the third party, they may still be liable to the third party for an agent's negligent misstatement if made within the scope of his actual or ostensible authority.

It has been contended that an estate agent acting for a vendor does not owe a duty of care to a purchaser as there would be a conflict between this duty and the duty he owes to his employer. The courts have not been persuaded of this view – it is said that the duty of honesty and accuracy does not conflict with the duty to the client. So the question of duty is determined on the facts of the case, applying the triple test.

Computastaff Ltd v Ingledew Brown Bennison & Garrett (1983)

The plaintiff sued his agents when he discovered that they had misinformed him about the rateable value of premises they had found for him to rent. He also sued his solicitors for not establishing the true value. The agents claimed to have relied upon information provided by the landlord's agents and so joined them as third party under the *Civil Liability (Contribution) Act* 1978. The landlord's agents claimed to have relied upon information provided by Westminster City Council (the valuation office) so joined them as fourth party. The judge expressed 'admiration for the dexterity with which each tried to pass the buck'. With the exception of Westminster City Council, the defendants were found to have acted negligently. It was held that the landlord's agents, if sued by the plaintiff tenant, could have been held liable under the *Hedley Byrne* line of authority. Therefore, they were liable as a contributor under the 1978 Act.

Where an estate agent reasonably believes that the advisee will rely on an independent inquiry, there is normally no duty of care.

McCullagh v Lane Fox & Partners Ltd (1996)

The plaintiff saw an advertisement offering for sale a house fronting the River Thames with gardens of nearly one acre. During a visit to the property, the vendor's estate agent confirmed the area of the gardens and the plaintiff was provided with a copy of the sale particulars which described the house as being set in 0.92 acres. The particulars also contained disclaimers, including:

> '... all statements contained in these particulars as to this property are made without responsibility on the part of Lane Fox ...'

Later in the visit the plaintiff informed the agent that if he bought the property he would demolish the house, keep the swimming pool, incorporate a tennis court and build a 'dream home'. After buying the property, the plaintiff discovered that the gardens were in fact only 0.48 acres and not large enough to accommodate a tennis court.

The Court of Appeal held that there had been no breach of duty under the rule in *Hedley Byrne*. Two of the judges thought there had been no duty of care because, at the time the agent made the oral statement confirming the size, he would have been entitled to take the view that his statement would be independently checked (by the plaintiff's solicitor or surveyor) and would not be relied upon. The judge at first instance had held that the duty of care arose as soon as the agent discovered that the plaintiff intended to demolish the house and rush through the transaction in two days, because at this point the agent would know that there would be no independent survey. The majority in the Court of Appeal disagreed, stating that one cannot correct a misrepresentation when one is not aware it is false. The third judge, on the other hand, was of the opinion that as soon as the agent knew that the plaintiff would not be relying on a survey, it was his duty to take reasonable steps to see that the plaintiff was not caused loss.

In any case, all three judges agreed that, whether there was a duty of care or not, the disclaimer operated to exclude liability. Its effect was to deny the assumption of responsibility necessary for liability under the rule in *Hedley Byrne* in respect of the written particulars and the oral statement. The disclaimer was also held to be fair and reasonable.

3.8.1 The use of disclaimers and the application of the Unfair Contract Terms Act 1977 in the context of negligent misstatements

In the rule in *Hedley Byrne* (as in the case itself), a disclaimer in appropriate terms will normally exclude liability as it shows that the maker of the statement has not assumed responsibility for it. However, disclaimers are now subject to the *Unfair Contract Terms Act* 1977 which, despite its title, applies to attempts to exclude liability in tort as well as in contract.

Under the heading 'Negligence Liability', section 2 provides:

'(1) A person cannot by reference to any contract term or to a notice given to persons generally or to particular persons exclude or restrict his liability for death or personal injury resulting from negligence.

(2) In the case of other loss or damage, a person cannot so exclude or restrict his liability for negligence except in so far as the term or notice satisfies the requirement of reasonableness.'

Section 11(3) provides:

'In relation to a notice (not being a notice having contractual effect), the requirement of reasonableness under this Act is that it should be fair and reasonable to allow reliance on it, having regard to all the circumstances obtaining when the liability arose or (but for the notice) would have arisen.'

The effect of section 2(2) coupled with section 11 is to require disclaimers in respect of liability in tort for economic loss to satisfy the test of reasonableness in the circumstances of the case.

Smith v Eric S Bush (1989)

A firm of valuers was instructed by a building society to carry out a mortgage valuation. The valuation was negligent, so the borrower, having relied on the report, sued for damages. The firm relied on a disclaimer of responsibility which had been signed by the borrower, but the House of Lords held that this disclaimer failed the test of reasonableness under the *Unfair Contract Terms Act* 1977. However, the House observed that it might be different in the context of commercial property and very expensive residential property.

McCullagh v Lane Fox & Partners Ltd (1996)

As noted above, the Court of Appeal took the view that, if there were a duty of care owed by the vendor's estate agent to the purchaser, it would be negated by the disclaimer that: 'all statements contained in these particulars as to this property are made without responsibility on the part of Lane Fox ...' for this indicates that there is no assumption of responsibility by the agent for the misstatement.

Furthermore, the contract with the vendor included the standard clause 'that the purchaser has not entered into this contract in reliance ... upon any statement ... by or on behalf of the vendor'. It would, therefore, be inconsistent for the purchaser to claim that he has relied on what the agent said whilst contracting that he has not. So the question for the Court was whether the disclaimers were fair and reasonable. In the circumstances, it was held that they were. Lord Justice Hobhouse observed that the purchaser was sophisticated and experienced. He had the sale particulars in his possession and was aware that they would contain a disclaimer. He could have chosen an independent check on the acreage. He could have interrogated the vendor through his own solicitor.

> 'The use of disclaimers to insulate the estate agent, and the estate agent's principals, from responsibility for representations made by estate agents is commonplace and is the normal basis upon which house sale transactions are carried out every day across the country.'

There was no basis for saying, in the context of the case, that it would be unfair to the plaintiff to allow the defendants to rely upon the disclaimer.

[**Note:** It is salutary for agents to note that the purchaser only had notice of the disclaimer because the vendor happened to give him a copy of the sale particulars, which carried the disclaimer, as he was leaving the house.]

Scope of disclaimer

The disclaimer must, of course, cover the advice given by the agent. Where, for example, advice is given to an intending purchaser in respect of a future transaction such as a resale, the disclaimer will be inoperative if it only relates to the actual sale.

Duncan Investments Ltd v Underwoods (1998)

The defendant agents were instructed to sell 16 properties for receivers. A partner of the agents showed the plaintiff the properties. The plaintiff expressed an interest in buying the properties with a view to reselling them individually at a profit. At the plaintiff's request, the partner told him what should be the asking price and the 'minimum achieve' price for each property. Subsequently, the defendants sent to the plaintiff sales particulars which included a printed disclaimer. Relying upon the partner's advice, the plaintiff purchased the properties but resold them at a substantial loss. The plaintiff sued the defendants for the loss in tort. The defendants relied upon the disclaimer. The disclaimer stated:

> 'Underwoods for themselves and for the vendors of this property whose agents they are give notice that ... the vendor does not make or give, and neither Underwoods nor any person in their employment has any authority to make or give any representation or warranty whatever in relation to this property.'

The judge at first instance held that Underwoods owed the plaintiffs a duty of care as the partner knew that the plaintiffs would rely on his advice and that it was unlikely that they would obtain independent advice (see *McCullagh v Lane Fox,* above, on this point). He also held that the disclaimer did not protect them. This second issue was appealed against, but the Court of Appeal affirmed the judge's decision. It was held that the disclaimer was limited to statements on behalf of the vendor in relation to the sale. It was not intended to cover statements by Underwoods in relation to a hoped-for future transaction by the intended purchaser. Therefore the defendants were liable.

Agent appointed by mortgagee or receiver

Where property belonging to a defaulting mortgagor is to be sold by the mortgagee or receivers, it will normally be put in the hands of selling agents or auctioneers. If they fail to market the property properly, the mortgagor cannot sue the agents direct under the rule in *Hedley Byrne* because there is no proximity of relationship. However, the mortgagor can bring an action in equity (not in tort) against the receivers (*Medforth v Blake),* or the mortgagee (*Cuckmere Brick Co v Mutual Finance Ltd)* for the negligence of the agent.

Raja v Austin Gray (2003)

Raja mortgaged properties to Development Finance Ltd (DF). DF, in turn, borrowed money from the Midland Bank, secured by a debenture. DF became insolvent and Midland Bank appointed receivers to realise DF's assets (acting as DF's agents). DF had become entitled to exercise a power of sale over Raja's properties, so the receivers instructed the defendant valuers to value Raja's properties. The properties were valued and sold for £245,000. Raja claimed that the properties had been undervalued. After he was tragically murdered, his wife brought an action in negligence against the valuers.

The Court of Appeal held that Raja could claim against the mortgagee (DF) and against the receivers in equity for the negligence of the agent. It was no defence for the mortgagee or receivers to say that they had entrusted the sale to apparently competent professionals. It was, therefore, unnecessary to impose a duty of care upon the valuers as well. There was no sufficient relationship of proximity. The borrower is not an advisee and did not act on advice given by the valuer, so although the foreseeability test had been satisfied, there was no relevant assumption of responsibility.

Peculiar nature of agency of receiver

Although a receiver appointed by a mortgagee is normally deemed to be the agent of the mortgagor (under the terms of the mortgage or the *Law of Property Act* 1925) this agency is of a special character which does not create the normal fiduciary duty of an agent to the principal. Like the mortgagee, the receiver can choose when to sell. Provided he acts in good faith, he is entitled to sacrifice the interests of the mortgagor in pursuing his primary duty – repayment of the debt.

Silven Properties v Royal Bank of Scotland plc (2003)

The appellant's properties were mortgaged to the respondent bank. The bank appointed receivers who sold the properties in exercise of the power of sale. Although several of the properties were development sites, the receivers decided not to apply for planning permission for the sites. The appellant claimed that the receivers were under a duty to pursue planning applications in order to achieve the best price obtainable.

The Court of Appeal held that the mortgage creates no ordinary agency and that general agency principles are of limited assistance in identifying the duties owed by a receiver to a mortgagor. The agency is peculiar in a number of respects including the fact that the mortgagor has no say in the appointment or identity of the receiver, cannot give the receiver any instructions, and cannot dismiss him. Furthermore, there is no contractual relationship or duty owed in tort. The receiver's primary duty is to get the debt repaid, he is not managing the property for the benefit of the mortgagor. So the receivers in this case were entitled, in the same way as the mortgagee, to sell the property in the condition in which it is.

4
Remuneration of the agent

4.1 EFFECT OF WORKING ON A COMMISSION BASIS

Agents who render services usually charge according to the time spent on such services. Agents who are employed to achieve a result, such as a sale, usually charge fees on a commission basis. Surveyors providing professional services fall into the former category. Estate agents fall into the latter category and so usually receive no remuneration for work done where the result has not been achieved.

> '[The principal's] only promise is that he will pay commission if the contract is completed. There is no promise to pay commission if the principal revokes the authority to the agent. And it is a further objection to a claim on a quantum meruit that the employer has not obtained any benefit. The agent has earned nothing until the event materialises.' (Lord Wright in *Luxor v Cooper.*)

Thus if a commission is to be payable before the result is achieved, it must be expressly provided in the contract.

Likewise, if an estate agent intends to charge a client for a valuation, it should be provided for in the contract.

Gross Fine & Krieger Chalfen v Clifton (1974)

Mr Justice Kilner Brown said:

> 'All the experts agree that if a person asked for a figure to be placed upon the property, the agent would not charge for that, but would expect to make his fee upon sale. A valuation which attracts scale fees is a matter of specific and special arrangement.'

In fact, such an arrangement was implied in the circumstances of the case but the judge awarded only half the scale fee.

[Note that the RICS scale of fees has been abolished, see 4.8.]

4.1.1 No implied term that principal must not deprive agent of commission

Where the agent has been instructed to find a purchaser and he introduces someone willing to purchase, there is no implied obligation on the principal to continue with the sale. There is therefore no breach of contract if the principal withdraws, so long as he has not entered into a binding contract with the purchaser.

Luxor (Eastbourne) Ltd v Cooper (1941)

The appellant companies wished to sell their cinemas and agreed to pay the respondent £10,000 commission on completion of the sale. The respondent introduced a willing and able purchaser, but the companies decided not to proceed with the sale. The respondent brought an action for breach of an implied term of the contract that the appellants would not, without just cause, act so as to prevent him earning his commission.

The House of Lords held that there was no such implied term. Terms are only implied in order to give business efficacy to a contract. Agents charge a high commission knowing that in some cases they will get nothing, particularly where multiple agents are employed. The risk of not obtaining any commission is part of the business. If the agent is not willing to run the risk he must include a clearly worded express term to protect him.

If, however, the principal had entered a binding contract with the buyer, then, in the view of Lord Russell of Killowen, a purchaser would have been introduced and commission would be due. Lord Wright expressed a similar view, although he stated that the principal would probably be in breach of the agency contract if he failed to complete.

[**Note:** The principles in *Luxor* apply equally whether the agent is acting for the buyer or seller.]

4.2 INTERPRETATION OF COMMISSION CLAUSES

It is clear from the *Luxor* case that no commission is due for 'finding a purchaser' until the agent has introduced a person who actually completes the purchase or, at the very least, enters a legally binding contract. Whether a person who has entered a contract can fairly be called a purchaser is not a simple matter, and subsequent cases have examined this question. Estate agents have also devised various commission clauses to protect them in the event of the client withdrawing at a late stage (or even at an early stage in some cases!) and the courts have been called upon to determine at what stage a person can be fairly described as 'prepared to purchase', 'ready, willing and able to purchase', or 'prepared to enter a contract', etc. This has proved a difficult issue for the courts and some of the judges have taken the view that commission clauses which depart from the 'common understanding' that commission is only payable on sale, must be brought to the attention of the signing party, otherwise they are not enforceable. This is not the view of the majority, who have taken a caveat emptor approach. The following selection of cases has been made with the intention of providing the reader with a good understanding of the modern judicial approach to commission clauses in general.

4.2.1 General principle

As noted above, the leading case of *Luxor v Cooper* makes it clear that no commission is due for finding a purchaser until the agent introduces a person who actually purchases. Commission or damages may also be due if the client vendor wilfully refuses to complete. However, it does not necessarily follow that commission cannot be earned for introducing someone who only reaches a pre-contract stage. So long as the terms are clear, an agent may be able to earn commission for something less than contract or completion.

> 'It is possible that an owner may be willing to bind himself to pay commission for the mere introduction of one who offers to purchase at the specified or minimum price, but such a construction of the contract would, in my opinion, require clear and unequivocal language.' (Lord Russell of Killowen in *Luxor v Cooper*.)

Lord Russell's statement laid down the gauntlet to agents who wasted little time in drafting commission terms that they hoped would meet his criteria of 'clear and unequivocal language'. There followed a series of cases in which the judges had to decide whether commission was due where something less than a sale had been achieved. This resulted in the evolution by judicial selection of standard phrases which successfully earned commission although no sale or even contract of sale had occurred. But it should not be assumed that each of the cases sets a precedent. It is now well established contract law that the meaning of a document must be construed having regard to the 'matrix of fact' in the case in question. This matrix includes:

> '… absolutely anything which would have affected the way in which the language of the document would have been understood by the reasonable man'. (Lord Hoffman in *Investors Compensation Scheme Ltd v West Bromwich Building Society.*)

So the words in a contract may have a different meaning in different circumstances. This principle shows how important the background facts of a case may be and should be borne in mind when examining any contract case law, let alone the controversial area of commission clauses in the following cases.

4.2.2 'Find/introduce a purchaser'

The use of the word 'purchaser' is normally taken by the courts to indicate that there must be at least a binding contract. (It may be different where a 'ready, willing and able purchaser' is required, see below.) And even this will not suffice if the intending buyer, being a person of no means, is unable to complete the transaction. Therefore the intending purchaser must be willing and able to complete the purchase.

Jones v Lowe (1945)

The defendant put her house in Maidenhead on the market through the plaintiff estate agent. A confirming letter stated 'in the event of my introducing a purchaser I shall look to you for payment of the usual commission'. The agent found a person ready and anxious to purchase the client's house. Before contracts were entered, the defendant withdrew the house from the market because house prices in towns outside the London area were rising as German bombing of London intensified.

The judge held, following *Luxor v Cooper*, that 'purchaser' does not mean somebody ready, willing and able to purchase, but a person who has purchased. This means he must have, at the very least, entered into a binding contract to purchase. Therefore no commission was due. Nor could there be any claim in quantum meruit (below) as this is inconsistent with the concept of payment for a result.

McCallum v Hicks (1950)

The agents were instructed by the defendant 'to find someone to buy my house'. A person was introduced who signed an agreement subject to formal contracts being drawn up. The defendant then withdrew from the transaction.

The Court of Appeal held that 'find someone to buy' meant 'find a purchaser'. Therefore commission was only payable when a binding contract for sale had been entered into.

Poole & Clarke & Co (1945)

The plaintiff signed a form instructing the defendant agents 'to find a purchaser' for his house. The agreement also authorised the agent to receive any deposit and to apply it, on signing of the contract, towards their commission of ten per cent and expenses. The defendants introduced someone who signed a legally binding contract to buy the plaintiff's house and paid £100 deposit to the defendants. This person turned out to be a 'man of straw'. He was unable to raise the money for the purchase and so forfeited his deposit. The plaintiff claimed the deposit, but the defendants contended that they were entitled to keep it as their commission, having found a purchaser.

The judge held that, even though a contract had been entered into, the agents had not found a purchaser. A purchaser is a person who is both willing and able to complete. It could not include a man of straw or a man without means.

Where a contract is entered into but completion does not take place because of wilful default of the vendor, the agent is entitled to commission. But wilful default means 'wilful refusal or deceit' (*Blake & Co v Sohn*).

Blake & Co v Sohn (1969)

The plaintiffs were instructed by the defendant vendors 'to do their best to introduce a purchaser for the property at £75,000 or to obtain an offer' in respect of an hotel with land at the back. The defendants did not own the land at the back, but claimed that they had a squatter's title. The plaintiffs introduced somebody who entered into a contract. However, this person successfully applied for rescission of the contract on the basis of a misrepresentation about the squatter's title. Relying on dicta in *Luxor v Cooper,* the plaintiffs claimed that a purchaser had been introduced when a binding contract had been made. Their answer to the defendants' response that no purchase had ever taken place because the contract was rescinded, was that this was the defendants' fault; they had not been able to provide good title.

The judge held that fault of the vendor means wilful refusal or deceit. The defendants' inability to complete was the result of an honest mistake. Therefore no commission was due.

4.2.3 Signing a binding contract

It has been seen that a purchaser may be said to have been introduced when a binding contract is entered into, so long as the purchaser remains ready and willing to complete the purchase. If he fails to complete, no commission is due unless the reason for the failure is the vendor's wilful refusal or deceit. However, if the agency agreement simply requires the agent to introduce someone who signs a legally binding contract, there is no additional requirement that that person remains ready and willing to complete. This is subject to the proviso that the agent has exercised reasonable care and skill in the introduction of the prospective purchaser. An agent who knowingly or carelessly introduces a 'man of straw' who cannot complete, will not be entitled to his commission, for the exercise of care and skill is an implied term of the agency contract.

Midgley Estates Ltd v Hand (1952)

The plaintiffs were instructed to dispose of a business, the Railway Supper Bar, commission to be paid 'as soon as our purchaser shall have signed a legally binding contract effected within a period of three months from this date'. The plaintiffs introduced a person who signed a binding contract to purchase and who paid a deposit. He was let into possession (for about 18 months) but the sale was never completed as he was unable to find the whole of the purchase price.

The Court of Appeal held that, according to the natural and reasonably clearly expressed meaning of the contract, the plaintiffs had earned their commission. It was unaffected by the subsequent fate of the contract of the sale. The words 'our purchaser', in the context, mean a person who contracts to buy, not a person who eventually completes the sale. The Court added that there was no evidence that the purchaser was a man of straw. There was good reason for believing that he would be able to complete. His inability to do so was partly due to the fact that the defendant was not disposed to advance on mortgage a part of the price.

Peter Long & Partners v Burns (1956)

The plaintiffs were engaged to sell the defendant's garage business. The agency agreement provided that commission was to be paid 'upon your introducing a person ready, willing and able to enter into a binding contract to purchase my business'. A prospective purchaser asked the agent if he knew of any town planning schemes. The agent, repeating information from the defendant, informed the prospective purchaser that some two or three feet would be taken from the front of the garage by the local authority. The prospective purchaser entered into a contract to buy the premises and paid a deposit. It transpired that the local authority's road widening scheme would necessitate the compulsory purchase of the bulk of the premises. So the prospective purchaser refused to complete. The agents claimed the commission on the basis that a binding contract had been entered into.

The Court of Appeal held that no binding contract had been made as it was not enforceable against the purchaser by reason of the agent's misrepresentation. Therefore no commission had been earned.

It was contended for the plaintiffs that, as the agent's statement was based on information provided by the defendant, it was the defendant's fault that the contract was not enforceable, and she should not be able to take advantage of that to deny liability to pay the commission. But the Court held that as the agent had not checked the statement he only had himself to blame. He must have known that, if the answer was incorrect, the sale could not go through.

Scheggia v Gradwell (1963)

The plaintiff instructed the defendant to find someone to buy his restaurant business, held under a lease. The terms of the agency agreement provided that commission was due 'if within three months any person introduced by the agents enters into a legally binding contract to purchase the said business and property ...'. The agent found a person who signed a contract and paid a deposit. The contract was subject to a standard condition that the landlord's consent was required. If the consent could not be obtained, the vendor (tenant) could rescind the contract. Unfortunately, the prospective purchaser's bank reference did not satisfy the landlord, and when the landlord asked for further references, he failed to provide them and withdrew from the purchase. The agents claimed commission, but the plaintiff contended that, as he was never in a position to enforce specific performance of the contract against the purchaser, it was not a legally binding contract.

By a majority, Lord Denning dissenting, the Court of Appeal held that the commission event had been satisfied. A legally binding contract had been entered into, as required by the agreement. Under the terms of the agreement, it was not necessary to establish that there was a purchaser in the sense of someone who completes the purchase, or someone who was ready, willing and able to complete. Even though specific performance was not available, the contract was a legally enforceable contract; the repudiation was a breach of the contract, and could be enforced by a claim in damages. It was distinguished from the case *Peter Long & Partners v Burns*, where the contract could neither be enforced by specific performance nor damages because of misrepresentation.

If it had been established that a man of straw had been knowingly or carelessly produced, the result would have been different. There is an implied term that an agent must act in good faith and exercise reasonable care and skill (*Keppel v Wheeler*). But no such evidence was provided.

Lester v Adrian Barr & Co Ltd (1962)

The agency agreement required the agent to find someone 'willing and able to purchase the [leasehold] business' and provided that commission was payable when the purchaser 'signs a binding contract for sale' or if the agents 'receive a deposit … from a person who does not withdraw the deposit within a period of thirty days'. The facts of the case resemble *Scheggia v Gradwell*, in that a person was introduced who signed a contract of sale, but he failed to provide satisfactory references for the landlord. In this case, however, no commission was due as the additional requirement in the agency contract to provide a person 'able to purchase' had not been met. The fact that a contract had been signed, and a deposit paid and kept for 30 days, was insufficient, according to the terms of the contract.

4.2.4 Phrases indicating preparedness, readiness, willingness and/or ability to purchase

After the decision in *Luxor v Cooper*, estate agents used various phrases to enable them to recover commission where a client pulled out after a suitable buyer had been found. Terms such as 'prepared to purchase', 'willing to purchase', 'willing and able', 'ready and willing', etc. were commonly used. In general, the courts have taken the view that an unqualified offer, that is an offer which, if accepted, will form a binding contract, is the minimum requirement to satisfy such terms. However, the exact moment when a person becomes prepared and able to purchase depends on the commission agreement and the circumstances of the case. In *Savills Land & Property Ltd v Kibble* (below), on the facts of the case a prospective purchaser was found to be a ready, willing and able purchaser, even though matters had not gone beyond subject to contract negotiations when the vendor withdrew.

Willing and able to purchase

Graham and Scott (Southgate) Ltd v Oxlade (1950)

The agency contract provided that commission would be payable 'in the event of our introducing a person or persons willing and able to purchase ...'.

The agents found a person 'anxious to purchase', who 'had continually raised her offer to meet the rising appetite of the [vendor]'. However, her offers were made 'subject to contract' and 'subject to satisfactory survey'. The vendor eventually sold to someone else, and the agents sued for their commission.

Overruling previous authority, the Court of Appeal held that the agent had not established that the bidder was a person willing to purchase. Where a bidder has only made a qualified or conditional offer, such as 'subject to contract' or 'subject to survey', he or she is free to withdraw at any time.

It might be different if the phrase 'subject to contract' was introduced, not by the bidder, but by the client. Lord Justice Cohen observed that it would not be fatal to the agent's case if the client accepted, subject to contract, an unqualified offer made by an intending purchaser.

Prepared to enter a contract to purchase

AL Wilkinson Ltd v Brown (1966)

The plaintiff was authorised to sell the defendant's leasehold greengrocer's shop. Commission was due 'in the event of your introducing ... a person prepared to enter into a contract to purchase at' an acceptable price. The plaintiff found a prospective purchaser who was willing to buy but could not sign the contract. Initially he was unable to sign because the landlord was not satisfied with his references. When, eventually, the landlord was satisfied, he was still unable to sign because he had not sold his own property.

The Court of Appeal held that 'prepared to enter a contract' means willing and able to enter it. The prospective purchaser was nearly prepared, but that was not enough to earn the agent's commission.

It should be noted that the agents were heavily criticised by the Court for their conduct. First, in touting for business – they had gone to the vendor, not she to them – and second, in getting the defendant to sign a commission agreement, two or three times normal commission, with extraordinary clauses purportedly entitling the agent to commission on revocation of instructions at any time! These were probably void and were not sued upon. The agents were also criticised for resorting to threatening the defendant with liability for commission if she did not go through with the sale to the person they had introduced.

Ready, able and willing to purchase

Dennis Reed Ltd v Goody (1950)

Agents were instructed by the defendant 'to find a person ready, able and willing to purchase the ... property for the sum of £2,825 or such other price to which I shall assent. Upon your introducing such a person I will pay you commission in accordance with the Incorporated Society's scale.'

A prospective purchaser signed a contract at an agreed price, but attached a condition that if any road charges were outstanding, the vendor would indemnify him. The vendor's solicitors drew up a draft contract with the proposed change, but then the prospective purchaser withdrew.

It was held that the prospective purchaser was not ready, able and willing to purchase at the material time. The prospective purchaser must be ready, able and willing up to the time when an enforceable contract was made or, alternatively, up to a time when the defendants refused to enter into such a contract.

[See *Savills Land & Property Ltd v Kibble* on the latter point.]

Christie Owen & Davies v Rapacioli (1974)

The defendant instructed estate agents to sell the lease and goodwill of a restaurant, and to quote a price of £20,000. The agents would be entitled to commission if they effected 'an introduction either directly or indirectly of a person ready able and willing to purchase'. A prospective purchaser offered £17,000 which the defendant agreed to accept. After a draft contract was approved by the prospective purchaser's solicitors, a contract was engrossed and signed by him and sent on to the defendant's solicitors together with the balance of the contract deposit of £1,850. The defendant then received a better offer and gazumped the prospective purchaser. The estate agents claimed their commission.

Reviewing the authorities, the Court of Appeal held that commission was due when the person introduced by the agent makes a firm offer on terms acceptable to the vendor. This was the case. A distinction was drawn between a case such as this and cases where the prospective purchaser makes a conditional or subject to contract offer, or where a person introduced withdraws. The result is that, under an agreement such as this, a vendor may be liable to pay more than one commission.

Ready, willing and able purchaser

Savills Land & Property Ltd v Kibble (1998)

Sole agents were engaged by the defendant to sell property in two lots. Lot 1 comprised farms, and Lot 2 comprised 56 acres of agricultural land. The commission agreement provided for full commission on the event of exchange of contracts, but for half commission:

> '… if a ready, willing and able purchaser is introduced to the property and terms are agreed for the sale in accordance with the client's instructions … and this must be paid if the Client subsequently withdraws and unconditional contracts for sale are not exchanged'.

This wording follows the required statutory explanation of the effect of introducing a ready, willing and able purchaser in the *Estate Agents (Provision of Information) Regulations* 1991 (below). The phrase 'ready, willing and able purchaser' was also defined in accordance with the 1991 Regulations as:

> '… prepared and able to exchange unconditional contracts for the purchase of the property.'

The agents introduced a prospective purchaser whose offer of £845,000 was accepted by the defendant, subject to contract. On the evidence it was found that there was no doubt that the purchaser was anxious to purchase the property. However, the vendor appeared to have second thoughts and began to alter the terms of the original offer. In particular he attached a condition that his brother, who farmed Lot 2, be given an agricultural tenancy and a protected tenancy of a cottage. The prospective purchasers agreed to allow the brother a short-term farm tenancy but sought vacant possession of the cottage as originally agreed. At this point, the vendor decided to withdraw Lot 2 altogether from the sale. So the purchaser offered a reduced price for Lot 1 which was not accepted and the whole transaction fell through.

The Court of Appeal held that the judge had been entitled to find that the agents had introduced a ready, willing and able purchaser and so had earned the half commission. Lord Woolf MR said:

'The clause in question is designed to provide protection to the plaintiff when they are sole agents whose instructions are withdrawn ... It would be unrealistic to interpret clause 5.1 in a way which means that the entitlement to that fee only arises immediately before contracts are exchanged, so that both parties have agreed the terms of the contract and are ready to exchange by applying their signature. The position has to be judged at an earlier stage when ... a vendor withdraws. At that time was the purchaser ready, willing and able to purchase the property by entering into the contract which it was presupposed by both parties would be drawn up for exchange?'

The evidence showed that the purchaser met this criterion.

It is interesting to consider whether the Court would have awarded Savills commission if the purchaser, tiring of the vendor's attempts to extricate himself from the terms of the original agreement, had withdrawn instead of the vendor. This point illustrates the conceptual difficulty of establishing exactly when somebody is ready, willing and able to purchase when the vendor is free to alter the terms right up until contracts are exchanged.

Implied term that no commission is due where the property has already been disposed of

It has been seen that where an agent introduces a person who signs an unqualified offer capable of being turned into a binding contract by acceptance, he will usually have complied with the requirement of finding somebody willing and able to purchase (or words to the like effect) so long as he remains willing and able, etc. However, this is subject to an implied term that no commission is due if the property has already been sold to, or contracts have already been exchanged with, another purchaser.

AA Dickson & Co v O'Leary (1980)

The vendor put his house in the hands of the plaintiff agents and other agents.

Negotiations ensued with two prospective purchasers – one through the plaintiff and one through other agents. Eventually the person introduced by the plaintiff signed an unconditional contract and returned it to her solicitors. On the following day the solicitors told the vendor's solicitors that they were ready to exchange, but were informed that contracts had been exchanged with another purchaser the previous day. The plaintiff claimed that a person ready, able and willing to purchase had been introduced as she had signed unconditional contracts.

The Court of Appeal held (following dicta in *EP Nelson & Co v Rolfe*, 1.3 above) that there was an implied term that commission would not be payable if the property had already been sold, or a binding contract had already been entered into, before the person ready, able and willing to purchase had been introduced. Exactly when the introduction of a person ready, able and willing occurs is not clear, but Lord Denning indicated it would be when the signed contract reached the solicitors, though Sir David Cairns was of the view that it is when the contract is despatched to the other side. But see *Savills Land & Property Ltd v Kibble*, above, on this point.

It is worth noting that Sir David Cairns attached some reservations to his judgment. He stated that there may be cases where two estate agents are entitled to commission, depending on the terms of the agency agreement, and approved what Lord Justice Orr had said in *Christie Owen & Davies v Rapacioli* (above) to this effect.

Effect of exchange of contracts where 'readiness', 'willingness', etc. is required

It may be thought that, once a binding contract has been made, the agent has completed his task of finding somebody 'willing' or 'ready' or 'prepared' or 'able' to purchase. Although this is true in most cases, it is not necessarily the case for the following reasons.

First, if commission is expressed to be paid out of the 'purchase money', the Court may infer that no commission is due until the purchase price is paid. In other words, there must be completion. (Other terms may also imply this.)

Second, if a purchaser who has entered a contract backs out, he ceases to be 'ready', or 'willing', or 'prepared' to purchase, so no commission is due, unless the reason he backed out is the vendor's wrongful act. Nevertheless, the agent will still be entitled to commission if the vendor obtains specific performance of the contract, because the purchase must then be completed. But the vendor is under no obligation to seek specific performance or damages for breach of contract. Failure to take such action is not vendor default.

Able and willing to purchase – commission five per cent of total purchase price obtained

Boots v E Christopher & Co (1951)

The plaintiff vendor instructed the defendant agents to find a buyer for his sub-post office and shop. The agents sent a letter to the plaintiff stating 'no commission is payable until a person who is able and willing to purchase upon terms agreed to by you has been introduced by us'. In a second letter, the agents stated that 'commission would be at the rate of five per cent of the total purchase price obtained'. The Court of Appeal found that both letters formed the agency contract.

The agents found a person who signed a legally binding contract and paid a deposit to them as stakeholders. This person, despite being able to complete the purchase, decided to repudiate the contract and instructed the agents to forward the deposit to the purchaser. The agents claimed to be entitled to deduct their commission from the deposit, so the vendor sued for the return of the deposit.

The Court of Appeal held that, as the commission was expressed to come out of the 'purchase price', and the person introduced was not willing to purchase at the proper time, no commission was payable unless it could be established that the plaintiff, by a wrongful act, had deprived the agents of the commission. The Court rejected the agents' claim that the plaintiff had a duty to bring an action for specific performance or damages; so no commission was due.

If an action for specific performance were brought, the agent would get his commission. The same would apply if the vendor obtained damages which included the amount of commission he has to pay.

Christie, Owen and Davies Ltd v Stockton (1953)

This case concerns the sale of a restaurant lease and goodwill. It raises an interesting point about the interpretation of the commission clause now that section 40 of the *Law of Property Act* 1925 has been repealed. Under this section an oral contract for the sale of land was unenforceable. Under the current law, set out in section 2 of the *Law of Property (Miscellaneous Provisions) Act* 1989, oral land contracts are not merely unenforceable, they are void.

In the Stockton case, commission was due 'should the owner withdraw after having accepted an offer to purchase by a person able and willing to enter into a formal contract'.

It was held that an offer, subject to contract, would not suffice. However, an unqualified offer which was accepted orally would entitle the agent to commission. In such a case there would be a contract which the vendor could withdraw from lawfully, as oral contracts were unenforceable.

Today, this arrangement creates no contract at all. Whether the client's oral 'acceptance' of the firm offer would entitle the agent to commission is doubtful. As there is no contract at all, arguably there is nothing for the owner to 'withdraw' from – so no commission is due. Furthermore, the courts normally regard the word 'offer' as meaning something the acceptance of which forms a contract.

Willingness, preparedness, etc. to enter a contract

Where commission is payable on the introduction of a person 'willing to enter a contract' or 'prepared to enter a contract', the test of willingness or preparedness is not that an actual contract has been entered into. The words are given their ordinary meaning.

Willing to sign a contract at an agreed price

Trinder & Partners v Haggis (1951)

The commission clause provided that:

> 'In the event of us being successful in introducing a person willing to sign a contract to purchase at an agreed price, you will pay us ... commission ...'.

The agents found a person who signed a contract at a price authorised by the vendor and paid a deposit. The vendor then decided not to sell and refused to sign his part of the contract.

The Court of Appeal held, by a majority, that commission was due as the terms of the commission agreement had been met. The purchaser had done all in his power to indicate that he was a ready and willing purchaser on the terms stated. The argument that 'willing to sign a contract' meant introducing a person who had signed an enforceable contract was 'over subtle'. The words covered the events in this case.

Prepared to enter into a contract on terms to which the vendor assents

Ackroyd & Sons v Hasan (1960)

Estate agents were instructed to find buyers for part of business premises.

They were to become entitled to their commission:

> '... in the event of our introduction of a party prepared to enter into a contract to purchase on ... terms to which [the vendors] may assent'.

The agents introduced prospective purchasers who eventually signed a contract which was sent to the vendors' solicitor. This followed many weeks of negotiations during which all the details of the agreement had been thrashed out and the solicitors for both sides had reached agreement. In the view of the Court of Appeal, the purchasers were, therefore, 'prepared to enter into a contract to purchase'. Unfortunately, it was not until the vendors' solicitor took the contract to the vendors to sign that they informed him that they wished to retain a small part of the premises for storage. Therefore the second element of the commission event was not satisfied because the vendors had not assented to the contract terms. So the Court of Appeal reluctantly held that no commission was due.

4.2.5 Other clauses

In the event of securing for you an offer of £x

Bennett, Walden & Co v Wood (1950)

The words 'securing for you an offer' means securing an offer which by acceptance would give rise to a contract. If its acceptance does not make a contract, it is not an offer in the contractual sense. Therefore, following *Graham & Scott (Southgate) Ltd v Oxlade*, an offer subject to contract was not sufficient for commission to become due, even where the vendor 'accepted' the offer. The acceptance of a subject to contract offer does not bind the offeror.

Offers subject to contract or other conditions

The cases establish that a conditional offer or contract is not normally enough to establish that a person is willing and able to purchase or enter a binding contract. However, if the commission agreement clearly and unequivocally provides that commission is payable on entering an agreement subject to contract, the commission is due when that event occurs. Furthermore such a term in a commission agreement does not appear to fall foul of the *Unfair Terms in Consumer Contracts Regulations* 1999 as it is a 'core term', i.e. the subject matter of the contract, and therefore outside the scope of the legislation. (However, unfair notice or termination requirements may be within the legislation, below.) A vendor should, in the words of

Lord Justice Ormerod in *Drewery v Ware-Lane* (below) 'examine with very great care an agreement which he signs in these circumstances'.

Drewery and Drewery v Ware-Lane (1960)

The defendant instructed the plaintiff to find a buyer for his leasehold house. The commission agreement provided that 'I agree to pay you commission – when a prospective purchaser signs your "purchase agreement" and I sign your "vendor's agreement"'. A copy of each of these agreements was attached to the commission agreement, and both were expressed to be subject to contract. The plaintiff found a prospective purchaser who signed the 'purchaser's agreement' at an agreed price. The defendant signed the equivalent 'vendor's agreement'. Nine days later the defendant informed the plaintiff that he had sold the property to someone else as no progress had been made on the sale. The plaintiff claimed commission and the Court of Appeal awarded it. The terms of the commission agreement had been fulfilled, and the *Luxor* test of 'clear and unequivocal language' had been satisfied. The term 'prospective purchaser' did not mean a person ready, willing and able to purchase as the defendant claimed. It simply means a person who has the question of buying the property in prospect or in contemplation and is prepared to make an offer with regard to it.

Vague terms

The court cannot give effect to commission terms that have no ascertainable meaning.

Introduction of a person willing to sign a document capable of becoming a contract

Jaques v Lloyd D George & Partners (1968)

The plaintiff put the sale of his café business in the hands of the defendant agents. The commission agreement provided for the payment of commission:

'... should you be instrumental in introducing a person willing to sign a document capable of becoming a contract to purchase at a price, which at any stage of the negotiations has been agreed by me.'

Before the agreement was produced for signature the agent told the plaintiff that: 'If we find a suitable purchaser and the sale goes through, you will pay us £250.' He then produced the agreement and, after striking out the sole agency clause (as agents had already been engaged), asked the plaintiff to sign it. The plaintiff did so. The agents introduced a person who signed an agreement expressly made subject to the landlord of the premises granting his licence to assign and the purchaser providing satisfactory references. Those references were not provided, the landlord gave no licence, and the deal fell through.

Two members of the Court of Appeal held that, although the purchaser entered a binding contract, no commission was payable as the commission clause was meaningless. A document capable of becoming a contract could be anything from a blank piece of paper to a contract with no signature on it. A majority also found that the agent had misrepresented the terms of the commission agreement anyway, and so it was not enforceable.

4.2.6 Estate Agents (Provision of Information) Regulations 1991 (SI 1991/859)

It has been seen that, with some notable exceptions, the judiciary have taken a caveat emptor approach to commission clauses. However, they have stated that commission terms which depart from the general understanding that commission is only payable for finding a purchaser must be clear and unequivocal to be effective. This is now buttressed by the *Estate Agents (Provision of Information) Regulations* 1991, made under section 18 of the *Estate Agents Act* 1979, which provide that certain key terms must be explained using the words in the regulations. So where the terms 'ready, able and willing purchaser', or words having a similar purport or effect, are used by an estate agent in the course of carrying out estate agency work, he must explain in writing the intention and effect of those terms to the client in the manner specified in the regulations, as follows:

> A purchaser is a 'ready, willing and able' purchaser if he is prepared and is able to exchange unconditional contracts for the purchase of your property.

> You will be liable to pay remuneration to us, in addition to any other costs or charges agreed, if such a purchaser is introduced by us in accordance with your instructions and this must be paid even if you subsequently withdraw and unconditional contracts for sale are not exchanged, irrespective of your reasons.

Obviously this statutory explanation follows the general judicial approach to the interpretation of ready, willing and able. It makes it clear that commission is due even if the client withdraws before exchange of contracts, so long as the purchaser was prepared and able to exchange unconditional contracts at the time of the client's withdrawal. As to when this may occur, it is a question of fact in the circumstances of the case; see *Savills Land & Property Co v Kibble*, above.

[**Note:** Note that the regulations also provide statutory explanations for 'sole agency' and 'sole selling rights', below.]

4.3   EFFECTIVE CAUSE

The agent earns commission by being the 'effective cause' (sometimes called 'efficient cause' or 'direct cause') of the commission earning event, whether that is a sale, or the introduction of somebody 'willing to purchase', or whatever the commission agreement provides.

The agent must be the direct or effective cause not just an indispensable cause. (The latter is usually referred to as a causa sine qua non by the judges.) For example, the agent may have contributed in some way to the introduction of a purchaser or tenant, but another factor is of more significance. A mere introduction may or may not suffice, depending on the circumstances of the case. (See *London Mews Co Ltd v Burney*, below.)

Before examining the cases, it is well to bear in mind that each case turns on its own facts and care should be taken in attempting to extract general principles. It is also important to note that even where an agent is the effective cause, he is entitled to no commission unless he is employed.

> 'In order to found a legal claim for commission, there must not only be a causal, there must be a contractual relation between the introduction and the ultimate transaction of sale.' (Lord Watson in *Toulmin v Millar*.)

Cases where tenant subsequently purchases the property

The early cases on effective cause often concern the situation where the agent has found a tenant who subsequently purchases the property. To substantiate a claim for commission on the sale, the agent has to establish both that he was employed to find a purchaser and that he effected the sale. Mere introduction of the tenant may not justify commission on an eventual sale.

Millar, Son & Co v Radford (1903)

The defendant employed the plaintiffs to find a purchaser, or failing a purchaser, a tenant. The plaintiffs introduced a person who took a seven-year lease and were paid commission accordingly. After the tenant had been in possession for about 15 months he bought the freehold from the defendant.

The defendant claimed this was the result of fresh and independent negotiations between himself and the purchaser.

The plaintiffs claimed the sale commission less the letting commission. They contended that they had a continuous retainer, not an alternative retainer, and that the only reason that the purchaser had not purchased originally was that he did not have the funds at the time. The judge found no evidence of a contract so the plaintiffs appealed.

The Court of Appeal dismissed the appeal. Lord Collins MR said that there must be a contract to find a purchaser or a continuous retainer; there was neither. He also stated that it was not sufficient merely to show that the agent's action was an indispensable cause (causa sine qua non). It was necessary to show that the introduction was an efficient cause in bringing about the letting or the sale.

Chain of causation

If the agent can show that there is an unbroken chain of causation from his introduction through to the transaction, he will usually have established that he is the effective cause. Whether there is a break in the chain is a question of fact. A break may occur because of delay or an intervening act of another. In some complex cases it may be difficult to draw the line and, as in *Coles v Enoch*, 'it is easy for judges to take different views'.

Coles v Enoch (1939)

The plaintiff had authority to find a tenant for the defendant's empty shop which was opposite Victoria station. The plaintiff telephoned the firm of Scott & Adickes about the shop, and gave the location as Victoria Street, a few doors from the cinema. Mr Adickes expressed interest but doubted whether his partner, Mr Scott, would agree to take the shop. So the plaintiff asked Adickes to try to find him another tenant. By chance, at the time of the conversation, a Mr Wilkie was in the room with Adickes. He was looking for similar premises. Adickes told him about the premises and said if Scott did not want them he would put Wilkie in touch with them. He deliberately did not reveal the exact location to Wilkie (in case Scott decided to take the premises) but simply said they were 'in Victoria'. Wilkie went to Victoria station to try and find the empty shop and located it. It had the defendant's name and address on a 'To Let' notice. He agreed a lease with the defendant. The plaintiff claimed commission on the basis of an unbroken chain of causation from himself through Adickes to Wilkie.

At first instance the judge, admitting some difficulty, agreed with the plaintiff's claim. The defendant appealed.

The Court of Appeal reversed the judge's decision. Lord Justice Scott agreed with the judge below that the case was near the line. However, he regarded Adickes as acting as a subagent when he was asked to find a tenant, and so his deliberate concealment of the exact location was deemed to be the act of the agent. Consequently the agent deliberately stopped short of finding a tenant, and the letting was due to the tenant himself.

Purchaser attends auction but buys subsequently

Where the eventual purchaser is introduced to the property by attendance at auction, in the absence of any break in the chain this may be regarded as the effective cause of the sale, even though the seller withdraws the property from sale and negotiates the sale himself. However, whether the auctioneer is entitled to commission depends on the terms of the agreement.

Green v Bartlett (1863)

The defendant authorised the plaintiff to offer the island of Herm for 'sale by public auction, or otherwise'. The property failed to reach the reserve so was unsold. A Mr Hyde attended the auction but did not bid as he had not seen the island. The plaintiff continued to try to find a purchaser but ten days after the auction the defendant wrote to the plaintiff saying he had withdrawn the island from sale for the present. At this time the defendant was negotiating with Hyde for the sale of the island, and eventually the sale to Hyde was completed. The plaintiff sought commission for the sale under the terms of the agreement which allowed for a private sale.

The Court took the view that as the purchaser attended the auction, the purchase must be taken as being brought about through the means of the plaintiff, and so he was entitled to commission.

Two-agent cases

Although the agent who makes the first introduction may have the advantage, it is not necessary to have made the first introduction in order to be the effective cause. It is a question of fact to be decided on the evidence in each case.

> 'If, however, he shows that he was the first to introduce the purchaser, and that a purchase followed, and if no other facts are established, then it may well be that the judge will infer that the plaintiff was the effective cause. It can therefore be said that the evidential burden in such a case passes to the defendant, whether the other agent or the vendor, to prove more facts which displace that inference. But, even in such a case, I do not think that the further facts which the defendant then has to prove must be such as to show that interest aroused by the first introduction has evaporated, that is to say, entirely disappeared. It will be a matter for consideration in each case as to how far the defendant has to go before he has displaced an inference which might arise from the mere fact of the introduction followed by the purchase.' (Lord Justice Staughton in *Chasen Ryder v Hedges.*)

> 'None of the cases indicate that it is legally possible, in the absence of an express or implied contract to that effect, for the court to apportion the agreed commission between the two agents on an equitable basis that each introduction was a contributory cause of the purchase by the person introduced. Neither side proposed that solution as a legally permissible (or even desirable) result in this case. It is a case of winners and losers, all or nothing.' (Lord Justice Mummery in *Egan Lawson v Standard Life Assurance Co.*)

Bow's Emporium Ltd v AR Brett & Co Ltd (1927)

The respondent agents were engaged by the appellant to find businesses for sale. The agents found a business that was likely to be sold, examined the premises, informed the appellant of their interview with the managing director, and handed over a copy of the balance sheet. Commission of two per cent was agreed if the transaction went through. Subsequently, the appellant informed the agents that they had gone off the idea of purchasing the business. Despite this, the appellant negotiated for the purchase of the business through a person who was the auditor of the business for sale as well as the appellant's business. The agents claimed their commission.

The House of Lords held that where an agent is employed to make inquiries about a particular business with a view to his employer's acquiring it, on the terms of his being paid a commission if business is transacted, and where the parties are brought together through his agency, he is entitled to commission, even where the actual purchase is ultimately effected through the intervention of another agent, provided that his services are really instrumental in bringing about the transaction. Viscount Dilhorne referring to a statement of Lord Chief Justice Erle in *Green v Bartlett* said:

> 'The question whether or not an agent is entitled to commission on a sale of property has repeatedly been litigated; and it has usually been decided that, if the relation of buyer and seller is really brought about by the act of the agent, he is entitled to commission although the actual sale has not been effected by him.'

Hartnell, Taylor, Cook v Bromwich (1982)

The plaintiffs' commission was payable:

> '... for our introducing, directly or indirectly, a person ready, able and willing to purchase the property for the asking price or such other price as may be agreed by you'.

The plaintiffs introduced a potential buyer to the defendant. Negotiations were conducted through the plaintiffs but shortly broke down and the potential buyer looked for properties elsewhere. A second agent re-introduced this person to the defendant and was able to persuade him to make a better offer than before. The sale went through and the second agent was paid commission. The plaintiffs, having made the first introduction, claimed commission too.

The Court of Appeal found that, on the facts, the ending of the negotiations between the buyer and the plaintiffs and the re-opening of the negotiations with the second agent constituted a break in the causal connection between the original introduction by the plaintiffs and the sale. It was not enough for the plaintiffs to have made the first introduction, as the commission agreement required them to introduce a person ready, able and willing to purchase. The buyer's willingness to purchase was effected by the second agent. So the first agent was not the effective cause.

John D Wood v Dantata (1987)

The plaintiffs' commission was due 'if we are successful in introducing a purchaser with whom a sale is completed'. The defendant vendor, a Nigerian prince, also instructed another firm of agents, Beauchamp Estates, whose commission was due 'in the event of our producing a successful purchaser'. The eventual purchaser, a Nigerian chief, used both the plaintiffs and Beauchamp as channels for inspecting and making bids, but kept each in ignorance of the other. Furthermore, the vendor did not realise that the bids were coming from the same person as the chief was acting through his company when bids were put through the plaintiffs.

Beauchamp made the first introduction of the chief to the property. About a month later, the plaintiffs re-introduced him to the property, although he deceived them into thinking he had not seen it before. The plaintiffs commenced negotiations with the chief. During these negotiations, the chief acted through the plaintiffs and not Beauchamp. The plaintiffs were informed by the vendor that he would accept £850,000 and their negotiations with the purchaser resulted in bids (from the chief's company) rising from £650,000 to £775,000. But at this point, the chief went back to Beauchamp, and the price was negotiated through them up to £800,000. This bidding was done in the chief's own name. Both the plaintiffs and Beauchamp claimed commission, so the vendor refused to pay either. Both claims were heard together.

Although initially attracted to the argument that this was a case where, on its unusual facts, two commissions were due, the Court of Appeal upheld the judgment at first instance to award the commission to Beauchamp only. Lord Justice Nourse said that 'introduce a purchaser' means introduce a person to the purchase. So the first acquaintance is not paramount as the purchaser must be led to the transaction. Consequently the Court did not attach conclusive weight to the first introduction, although it could not be ignored as it generated the lively interest of the purchaser. The plaintiffs managed to get the purchaser up to the £775,000 mark, but what they did not do was to get him up to the £800,000 price agreed. As that was the achievement of Beauchamp, they were the effective cause.

The statement that the purchaser must be led to the purchase must be read in the context of this somewhat peculiar, two-agent case. (See *London Mews Co Ltd v Burney* on this point (below).) It is well worth noting that Lord Justice Nourse said that because the case was unusual 'I do not think that our decision is likely to be of any general application.'

Lordsgate Properties v Balcombe (1985)

It is rare for two agents to be regarded as the effective cause, but in the peculiar circumstances of this case, the judge found that both were entitled to commission.

Here the defendant instructed sole agents to sell his property. Notwithstanding this, he also instructed other agents, including the plaintiffs. The purchaser was first shown around the property by the plaintiffs, he visited again through the sole agents, and put in a bid through the sole agents, which was rejected. He then put a bid of £160,000 through each agent. Owing to a misunderstanding, the agents believed that these bids were from different bidders. So, at the behest of the defendant, a third party was gazumped, a contract race was entered and the purchaser bid £165,000 (against himself!) through the sole agent.

The plaintiffs' task was to 'introduce an applicant who purchases'. The judge found that as the plaintiffs introduced the purchaser and the chain of events was added to, not broken, by the work of the sole agents, they remained an effective cause. The sole agents were also entitled to their commission as they had fulfilled the terms of their commission agreement, which was to be 'instrumental in negotiating a sale'.

This may be regarded as a somewhat unusual approach, but the conduct of the defendant seems to have been a material fact too, for the judge also remarked that it was the defendant's actions, in gazumping and using two agents to help him bid up the price, that brought about the unusual situation of liability for two commissions. So the consequential loss of part of the increased price was, he said, 'fair and just'.

Glentree Estates Ltd v Gee (1981)

The plaintiffs were given a sole agency contract by the defendant for two months and introduced the eventual purchaser. No agreement was reached with this purchaser because the asking price, set by the defendant, was too high. The defendant then purported to terminate the sole agency agreement and instructed another agent. (The judge found that this was a breach of the agency contract.) The asking price was reduced and the second agent re-introduced the purchaser. The sale was completed, the second agents were paid a proportion of the commission (after a dispute) and the plaintiffs claimed their commission too.

The judge found that the plaintiffs were the effective cause of the sale. The chain of causation was not broken on the facts of the case, and the effective cause of the sale was the original introduction by the plaintiffs.

Egan Lawson Ltd v Standard Life Assurance Co (2001)

In September 1997, the plaintiff agents approached the defendant with information about a property they knew was coming on the market. (They were not retained by the vendor.) The defendant was not interested in purchasing the property as the asking price was too high. The plaintiffs played no further part. After the property was formally marketed in October by Savills, the retained agent, Richard Ellis approached the defendant and provided details about the property. Richard Ellis also provided a purchase report for the defendant and submitted a lower offer than the asking price. A sale was completed and the defendant agreed to pay Richard Ellis commission of one per cent. The plaintiffs sought commission, but their claim was rejected by the Court of Appeal. It was held that the transaction had nothing to do with the plaintiffs' introduction and would have occurred had there been no introduction by them at all.

Mere introduction may be sufficient

A mere introduction will suffice in a straightforward case, otherwise a vendor could avoid paying commission if a purchaser, having seen a 'For Sale' sign erected by the agent, knocked on the vendor's door and proceeded to deal directly with him instead of through the agent.

London Mews Co Ltd v Burney (2003)

The claimants entered a sole agency agreement with the defendant vendor. The agreement used the standard form of words set out in the *Estate Agent (Provision of Information) Regulations* 1991 (below at 4.5.1) which provides for commission for the introduction of a purchaser during the period of sole agency, whether introduced by the sole agent or another agent. The claimants prepared particulars of the defendant's property and advertised it in the press. A second agent, Kaye & Co, saw the advertisements and asked for a copy of the particulars for circulation to their clients. The claimants supplied the particulars but did not appoint Kaye as their subagents. Kaye then put the particulars on their own headed paper. A prospective purchaser, not retained by Kaye, saw the particulars and told Kaye that he wished to view the property. Kaye informed him that they were not retained by the vendor but said they could get him into the property if he agreed to pay a commission of one per cent. The purchaser expressed dissatisfaction with this way of doing business and did not agree to pay the commission. He was informed by Kaye that he could gain access to the property through the estate agents employed by the vendor, or by making his own private enquiries. Kaye would not inform him who the agents were, so he wrote to the vendor and proposed saving commission by dealing directly. During negotiations, the vendor wrote to the claimants stating that he was taking the property off the market. After a sale was agreed, the claimants found out about it and claimed commission. The vendor denied liability on the ground that the chain of causation was broken: first because the introduction by the second agent was made without authority; second because the purchaser was not put in touch with the claimants. So the claimants had not introduced a purchaser as they did not 'lead' the purchaser to the transaction, applying the words of Lord Justice Nourse in *John D Wood v Dantata*. Two of the judges in the Court of Appeal had little difficulty with either claim. First, in circulating the particulars, the plaintiffs had not done anything they were not entitled to do. So the case of *John McCann v Pow* (above) in which the second agent was appointed as a subagent without authority, could be distinguished. It was clearly the work of the claimant in preparing the particulars that had introduced the purchaser. Second, the words of Lord Justice Nourse were used in the context of two agents, in a rather peculiar case, competing for one commission, and were not to be extrapolated from as a basis for claiming that a mere introduction was insufficient to earn commission. If that were the case 'It would ... drive a coach and horses through the agreements which all estate agents make with vendors'. It would mean, using the example of Lord Justice Kay, that an agent would be denied commission where a person, having seen the agent's 'For Sale' sign, knocked on the door of the purchaser and then proceeded to negotiate a sale privately with the vendor.

The third judge, Mr Justice Lindsay, had difficulty distinguishing the *John McCann* case and decided the issue on a different ground, albeit in favour of the claimants. The facts of *John McCann* are very similar, except that the second agent was employed as a subagent. In that case, Lord Denning stated that the introduction of the purchaser was not made by the plaintiff estate agents. The basis of his judgment was that the introduction was made by the subagent, but without authority. So Mr Justice Lindsay states:

> 'If what had been done by McCann in that case did not suffice to amount to the introduction of a purchaser, I have difficulty in seeing why the extremely comparable acts done by [London Mews] in this case could suffice.'

So he turned to the alternative basis of claim that, under the terms of the sole agency agreement, introduction by another agent during the period of agency entitles the agent to commission. So the claimants won whether they were the effective cause or not.

[**Note:** It may be observed that the finding in *McCann* that the subagent made the introduction was not in issue in that case. The agents based their claim on different grounds. See 1.2.4 above.]

Introduction to the vendor

Actual introduction of the purchaser to the vendor is not normally necessary. It is sufficient if the agents introduce the purchaser to the property.

Christie Owen & Davies plc v King (1998)

The agency agreement provided for remuneration if a purchaser was 'introduced to you' during the period of agency. The agent provided details of the property to the eventual purchaser. After the agency contract was terminated, the purchaser contacted the vendor direct and they negotiated a sale. The Court dismissed the vendor's contention that the purchaser was not introduced to him. It was held that a personal introduction was not required where the agent introduces the purchaser to the property or brings him into a relationship with it.

Negotiation by the client or another agent

The *London Mews* case shows that an introduction will not cease to be the effective cause merely because the client conducts the negotiations himself. This is the application of the general principle set out in *Bow's Emporium Ltd v AR Brett & Co Ltd* (above) that, so long as the first agent is instrumental in bringing about the transaction, the introduction of another agent or go-between does not deprive the first agent of his legal rights.

Aylesford & Co (Estate Agents) Ltd v Al-Habtoor (2003)

A sole agency agreement was entered into between the parties. It provided for an initial three-month period which was to be continued after expiry of the three months until terminated by 14 days' written notice by either party. During the continuation period, a potential purchaser saw the claimant agent's advertisement and was shown around the defendant's property. The purchaser employed an acquaintance as a middleman between himself and the defendant. The middleman conducted viewing and negotiations which brought about the eventual sale.

The agent claimed commission and the Court awarded it. The fact that the purchaser used the services of the middleman did not undermine the agent's introduction. To the contrary, it arguably reflected the efficacy of the introduction.

Effect of termination of agency between introduction and sale

It is not uncommon for a client to terminate the agency contract after the agent has introduced a prospective purchaser and then to deny any liability for commission when an eventual sale to that purchaser takes place. (See, for example, *Green v Bartlett*.) Whether commission is due depends, of course, on the terms of the agency agreement, but if the agent is the effective cause and has complied with the contract, the vendor 'could not defeat his rights to commission by determining his employment before the sale was effected'. (Lord Watson in *Toulmin v Millar*.) See 1.3, above, on termination.

Christie Owen & Davies (t/a Christie & Co) v Jones (1966)

The plaintiff agents were employed by the defendant to introduce a purchaser of the defendant's inn for £25,500. The agents introduced a husband and wife who were extremely interested in purchasing the inn, but would not be able to do so until they had sold their own hotel. Some months later, the defendant terminated the agency agreement and informed the plaintiffs that he was going to withdraw the inn from the market. A few weeks after this, the husband and wife team who had expressed interest in buying the inn, sold their hotel and telephoned the defendant asking if the inn was still for sale. Upon being told that it was, negotiations ensued and they bought the inn for £26,000. When the plaintiffs found out, they claimed commission from the defendant. He claimed that no commission was due because the sale took place after the agency was terminated and, in any case, the plaintiffs were not the effective cause. Having referred to the authorities, including the observations of Lord Watson in *Toulmin v Millar*, Mr Justice Mocatta awarded judgment to the plaintiffs.

On the question of effective cause, the judge held that this is largely a question of fact. The defendant's argument was that as the purchasers were unable to raise the finance at the time, all negotiations ceased in July and were only resumed in January because the finance became available on the sale of their hotel. The introduction, claimed the defendant, was a mere sine qua non but not the direct or effective cause. The judge did not accept this argument. The delay pending the sale was not so excessive as to deprive the introduction of its operative effect, and the provision of finance through the sale of the purchasers' property was ordinary in character and in no way due to any activity on the part of the defendant.

4.3.1 Imposition of further conditions

Even though an agent may be the effective cause of the introduction of a person who completes a purchase, the agency contract may impose other preconditions on commission, such as time limits. If these are not satisfied, no commission is due.

Fairvale Ltd v Sabharwal (1992)

The defendants instructed the plaintiff estate agents to submit property for auction. Commission was due if a sale of the property, whether arranged by the auctioneers or not, was effected within 28 days after the auction. The property was not disposed of at the auction (it did not reach the reserve) but immediately afterwards the plaintiffs introduced the defendants to an unsuccessful bidder. This introduction resulted in a sale to the bidder, but it took place outside the 28-day period. No commission was due. Neither were the plaintiffs entitled to a quantum meruit payment, for it would mean rewriting the bargain made.

[Compare *Green v Bartlett*, above.]

4.3.2 Words displacing requirement of effective cause

Although the agent must normally be the effective cause in order to earn his commission, this can be displaced by clear words to the contrary. Furthermore, there is no reason in principle why an agreement should not provide for payment of commission on the mere introduction of a person, so long as the agreement is clearly worded. (See introductory fee agreements at 4.3.4 below.)

Tredinnick v Browne (1921)

The plaintiff estate agent was appointed sole agent for the sale of the defendant's property. Mr Justice Swift found the contract to be that the plaintiff should not only be appointed sole agent, but also that he should receive a commission whether he introduced the purchaser or not. He said:

> 'If two men, A and B, like to make a bargain that A shall pay B £500 if A's estate is sold, whether B has anything to do with the selling of it or not, then, if the estate is sold, A must pay.'

In an action for commission, judgment was given for the plaintiff.

Brian Cooper & Co v Fairview Estates (Investments) Ltd (1987)

The defendant landlord wrote to the plaintiffs stating that they were:

'... pleased to offer a full scale letting fee to your company should you introduce a tenant by whom you are unable to be retained and with whom we have not been in previous communication and who subsequently completes a lease'.

Later the defendants agreed to pay double commission on similar terms. The plaintiffs introduced a company, but that company then decided it did not need the property. Subsequently, the company altered its plans and was re-introduced to the property through its own retained agents. The plaintiffs played no part in this and it was agreed that they were not the effective cause. Nevertheless, the plaintiffs claimed commission as they had satisfied the requirements of the commission agreement. The defendants claimed that there was an implied term to the effect that the agents had to be an (or the) effective cause. The Court of Appeal held that the language of the clause was inconsistent with such an implication, and there was no necessity in this case to imply a term. The clause worked perfectly satisfactorily from a developer/landlord point of view.

[**Note:** By the time the case came to Court, Fairview had wisely altered their commission terms to include the requirement of effective cause.]

Effective cause and sole agency

Sole agency agreements usually provide for the payment of commission if, in breach of contract, another agent is instructed to find a purchaser to whom the property is sold. Similar provisions in sole selling agreements apply where the client, in breach of contract, finds someone who buys the property. Therefore commission may be due although the sole agent is not the effective cause. (For cases on sole agency and sole selling rights, see 4.5 below.)

4.3.3 **Negotiation**

An agreement may require the agent to negotiate a sale or purchase with a person already introduced. If so, the sale or purchase must be effectively caused by the negotiations for the agent to earn the commission. Furthermore, the agent must actually negotiate and not be a mere channel of communication. However, a claim on quantum meruit may be made for work done (see *Debenham Tewson & Chinnocks v Rimington* below).

FP Rolfe & Co v George (1969)

The defendant grocer instructed the plaintiff to find a buyer for his business. The plaintiff sent him the RICS scale of charges, which included fees for 'negotiating a sale by private contract, or introducing a person able, ready and willing to purchase on terms authorised by the vendor'.

A purchaser was introduced by a wholesaler (who was not seeking commission) so the defendant asked the plaintiff to help in the negotiations. The parties and the agent met to negotiate terms. The agent produced the accounts and took part in the negotiations. A deal was concluded and the agent sought commission on the sale. The defendant resisted on the ground that he had not introduced the purchaser. Lord Denning MR said of the agent's terms of business 'Those words mean ... that the agent must be, by reason of his negotiation, the efficient cause of the sale'. As there was clear evidence that this was the case, the agent had earned his commission.

Hoddell v Smith (1976)

The plaintiffs claimed scale fees for 'negotiating a sale by private contract'. (Another agent had introduced the buyer.) It was held by the Court of Appeal that advising the client on values and tactics is not negotiating.

> 'Negotiation must, to my mind, mean conferring with the prospective purchaser, or his representatives, with a view to agreeing a sale.' (Lord Justice Geoffrey Lane)

On the evidence, the agent had not negotiated a sale. The only communication with the purchasers or their representatives comprised letters, which did no more than pass on information from the client, and a meeting at which the agent played a very small part, if any part at all.

Debenham Tewson & Chinnocks v Rimington (1990)

The plaintiffs were to be paid 1.5 per cent commission for negotiations with developers for the sale of successive areas of land owned by the defendants, who were trustees of the Portsmouth Settled Estates. The plaintiffs were instructed to discuss values with the agents of the Grainger Trustees, as Grainger were interested in buying land from the defendants. There was a close relationship between Portsmouth and Grainger, so it was not a normal vendor purchaser case where each party was trying to negotiate the best price. The plaintiffs discussed values and comparables with Grainger's estate but were not authorised to put forward any offers. It was more in the nature of a preliminary exchange of views. They asked for instructions to agree a value, but Portsmouth never gave them any. Subsequently, Portsmouth and Grainger agreed a price themselves, the land was sold for approximately £32.5m and the plaintiffs claimed their 1.5 per cent commission.

The Court of Appeal held that the defendants' instruction to the plaintiffs to discuss values with Grainger's agent was not an instruction to negotiate with developers for sale, in accordance with the agency agreement. In any event, what had taken place – a discussion as to price – even if it could be called a negotiation, did not amount to negotiations for the sale of land within the meaning of the agreement. The plaintiffs were awarded £15,000 on a quantum meruit basis for the work done in discussing prices and comparables with Grainger's agent, rather than the £564,450 they claimed in commission.

4.3.4 Introductory fee agreement

This is an agreement under which the client agrees to pay a fee to the agent for the mere introduction of a prospective buyer or seller. Payment of the fee is conditional on the person introduced subsequently entering a sale or purchase, but the agent is not retained to negotiate and is entitled to the fee even though he may not be the effective cause. In cases such as this, the agent is usually seeking to be instructed, so it is important that the information is not provided before a contract is entered into (see *Lady Manor Ltd v Fat Cat Café Bars Ltd* below). It must also be made clear that the mere introduction, if taken up, will entitle the agent to commission, otherwise the Court will only award commission to the agent who was the effective cause.

Sinclair Goldsmith v Minero Peru Commercial (1978)

The defendants were looking for offices to rent in London. The plaintiff agents, who were not retained, met the defendants and took instructions to find appropriate property. The plaintiffs introduced a property to the defendants, but the rental was too high. Subsequently a retained agent for the property re-introduced the defendants to the property and was able to negotiate a lease at a lower rental. The plaintiffs claimed commission for introducing the property in the first place. The judge stated that in order to be entitled to commission for an introduction (which resulted in a deal) it is necessary to say so in clear terms. He found that the agreement was really for 'seeking and negotiating' and, although the plaintiffs were entitled to a sum for seeking, they were not entitled to full commission as they had not negotiated the tenancy.

Cold calling and cold mail

Where unrequested information is provided in the hope of a commission if a transaction ensues, there is no contract. The recipient can use the information without obligation. If an unretained agent wishes to obtain commission for imparting information, it is necessary to agree beforehand that a fee is due for the disclosure of the information and in the event of a transaction ensuing.

Lady Manor Ltd v Fat Cat Café Bars Ltd (2001)

The claimant estate agent sent a letter to the defendant ('cold mail') with information about a property that the claimant thought the defendant might be interested in acquiring. The claimant was not retained by the vendor. The letter set out the fee payable to the claimant in the event that the introduction led to a successful transaction. The defendant, believing that the claimant was retained by the vendor, asked his own agent to arrange to view the property. This resulted in a sale of the property to the defendant, so the claimant sought commission.

The county court judge held that no commission was due. Conferring an unrequested benefit cannot require payment to be made, otherwise a contract could be imposed upon the recipient. The information provided was past consideration. For a contract to be created, there would need to be a promise of further information in return for a fee. On the facts, the letter was ambiguous and was not a clearly expressed offer of further information which could be accepted by the defendant.

Egan Lawson Ltd v Standard Life Assurance Co (2001)

A non-retained agent wrote to the defendant providing information about a property that was coming on the market. The letter said: 'I look forward to discussing the matter further and confirm that we would wish to act for you for a fee based on one per cent of the purchase price plus VAT'. The defendant was not interested as the price was too high. Subsequently a second non-retained agent re-introduced the property to the defendant and facilitated a deal by establishing that the vendor would sell at a lower price. It was held that the first agent was not the effective cause.

Commenting on the nature of the agreement in this case, Lord Justice Simon Brown distinguished between a case where a vendor instructs agents and a case such as this where the agent is asking to be instructed. It is, he said, entirely a matter for the purchaser as to whether to contract with the agent and, if so, on what terms. In the absence of clear terms, one could not regard the prospective purchaser as agreeing to pay a fee, provided only that he eventually purchases the property in question; the standard basis upon which a vendor instructs his agent to find a purchaser. In his view, even if the second agent were not entitled to commission (he doubted that they were, although eventually the defendant agreed to pay commission) it would have made no difference to the plaintiffs' claim.

4.4 TERMINATION

Termination is a matter for the parties, see 1.3, above.

Whether an agent is entitled to remuneration after the agency agreement is terminated depends on the agreement. A sole agency agreement, for example, may provide that commission is due in respect of introductions made during the period of sole agency even though the sale does not take place until after the agency contract has expired (below).

Where there is no such provision, it is well established that a principal cannot avoid paying commission by simply terminating the agency between the introduction and the eventual sale (*Toulmin v Millar*).

Christie Owen & Davies (t/a Christie & Co) v Jones (1966)

The claimant agents introduced a prospective purchaser who was unable to purchase at the time. The defendant terminated the agency and subsequently proceeded to negotiate a sale with the person introduced by the agents who was now in a position to buy. The agents claimed commission and were awarded it. Mr Justice Mocatta observed that if an agent could be deprived of commission merely by termination of the agent's mandate:

> '... it would be necessary for estate agents always to protect themselves against such an easy way of depriving them of their remuneration by stipulating that their mandates should be irrevocable for specified and probably rather substantial periods of time.'

EP Nelson & Co v Rolfe (1949)

The Court of Appeal held that there is an implied term that the estate agency is terminated in the following events, so long as they take place before the agent fulfils his contract by finding a purchaser:

- when the agent's authority is withdrawn;
- when the property is sold;
- when a binding contract of sale is made.

4.5 SOLE AGENCY AND SOLE SELLING RIGHTS

Under a sole agency agreement, the client agrees not to instruct another agent during the period of sole agency. Instruction of another agent would then be a breach of contract, but it is no breach of a sole agency contract for the principal to sell the property himself. Only if the sole right to sell is clearly conferred upon the agent would the principal be in breach.

Chamberlain & Willows v Rose (1924)

The defendant cinema owner put his property in the hands of the plaintiff estate agent on the following terms:

> 'The property to be left solely in your hands for sale from this date until the auction and for a further period of three months.'

The defendant sold the cinema himself. The Court held that no commission had been earned, because the agent had not found a buyer. But it also held that the defendant was in breach of contract as the words 'solely in your hands' meant that the agent had the sole right to sell. The Court remitted the case to the county court, observing that damages for breach might be far less than the commission as the plaintiffs might not have been able to sell the property, or might have got only a very small sum for it.

Bentall, Horsley and Baldry v Vicary (1931)

The defendant appointed the plaintiffs his 'sole agents for the sale of the property' for a period of six months. The defendant found a buyer himself. The buyer had had no contact with the plaintiffs, and was not even aware that they were the agents.

The Court held that clear words are required to confer the sole right to sell. The words in the contract only conferred sole agency, and there was no implied term to the effect that the defendant could not sell the house himself. Therefore there was no breach of contract.

Property Choice Ltd v Fronda (1991)

One of the clauses of a 'sole agency agreement' provided that, until the agreement was terminated, the defendants 'will not consent to sell the property to anyone not introduced by Property Choice'. The Court of Appeal held that the clause plainly and clearly created a sole selling agreement. The argument that this was inconsistent with the description of the plaintiffs as sole agents was not accepted. The meaning of the agreement had been explained to the clients and a copy had been left with them.

4.5.1 Estate Agents (Provision of Information) Regulations 1991 (SI 1991/859)

Wording of sole agency and sole selling rights agreements

Where the terms 'sole selling rights' and 'sole agency', or terms to the like purport and effect, are used by an estate agent in the course of carrying out estate agency work, the intention and effect of those terms must be explained in writing having the form and content specified in the regulations. However, if the statutory explanation would be misleading because of the provisions of the contract, the explanation shall be altered so as to accurately describe the liability of the client to pay remuneration.

The statutory explanations are as follows:

Sole selling rights
You will be liable to pay remuneration to us, in addition to any other costs or charges agreed, in each of the following circumstances–

■ if unconditional contracts for the sale of the property are exchanged in the period during which we have sole selling rights, even if the purchaser was not found by us but by another agent or by any other person, including yourself;

■ if unconditional contracts for the sale of the property are exchanged after the expiry of the period during which we have sole selling rights but to a purchaser who was introduced to you during that period or with whom we had negotiations about the property during that period.

Sole agency

You will be liable to pay remuneration to us, in addition to any other costs or charges agreed, if at any time unconditional contracts for the sale of the property are exchanged–

■ with a purchaser introduced by us during the period of our sole agency or with whom we had negotiations about the property during that period; or

■ with a purchaser introduced by another agent during that period.

Interpretation of statutory explanations

According to the statutory explanation of sole agency, the agent need not make the introduction himself to earn commission. So long as the introduction is made by another agent during the period of agency, commission will be payable if the person introduced exchanges contracts. This is because an instruction to another agent is in breach of the sole agency contract and threatens the agent with loss of commission. However, the wording of the statutory explanation of sole selling rights is different, and the judicial interpretation is that the introduction must be made by the agent where contracts are exchanged after expiry of the period of sole selling rights.

Michael Harwood t/a RSBS Group v Smith (1998)

The plaintiff estate agent was instructed by the defendant vendors to find a purchaser for a residential home. The agreement gave the plaintiff sole selling rights for six months. The sole selling rights explanation in the *Estate Agents (Provision of Information) Regulations* 1991 was incorporated into the contract. The agreement also expressly precluded the defendants from offering the property privately. The defendants, responding to a newspaper advertisement, found a purchaser themselves, and exchanged contracts with the purchaser two days after the sole selling rights agreement expired. The plaintiff claimed commission on the basis that the purchaser had been, in the words of the explanation, 'introduced to you' during the period of the sole selling agreement. However, the Court of Appeal held that the words 'by us' were implied after the words 'introduced to you'. Therefore no commission was due.

The Court of Appeal noted that the first paragraph of the statutory explanation, dealing with exchange of contracts **during** the period of sole selling rights, provides for commission 'even if the purchaser was not found by us but by another agent or by another person including yourself'. The wording is comprehensive. But in the second paragraph, concerned with exchange **after** the agreement has expired, the words 'introduced to you' are not so qualified and are followed by the words 'or with whom we had negotiations about the property during that period'. The Court took the view that the second paragraph would be 'reasonably understood by a client' as providing for commission where either (a) the agent introduces the purchaser, or (b) the agent does not introduce the purchaser but negotiates with him. If this were not the case and commission becomes due if the purchaser is introduced by another agent, there would be no point in including part (b); the commission would be payable anyway. The Court observed that, given the purpose of the regulations to bring home clearly to the client when he would be liable for commission, the explanation 'does not make it clear that he is still to pay commission in respect of an exchange of contracts outside the period when the introduction was not effected by the agent'. Furthermore, the argument that the statutory wording should be construed in the context of the explanation of sole agency is of little relevance to a contract in which the other explanation does not appear.

Observations on the impact of the Harwood case

As stated above, the statutory explanation of sole agency expressly provides for commission to be due in the event of another agent introducing a purchaser during the period of sole agency, regardless of when exchange of contracts takes place. But the judicial interpretation in the *Harwood* case results in agents with sole selling rights being at risk of losing the commission where another agent introduces the purchaser. Consequently, agents with sole selling rights appear to be in a weaker position in this respect than sole agents. An action for damages for breach of contract would be available but such damages may be less than the full commission. (See 4.5.2, below, on damages for breach of sole agency agreements.)

Meaning of 'introduced to you'

Where an agent with sole selling rights has introduced the purchaser to the property during the agency agreement, the vendor cannot deny liability to pay commission on the basis that there was no personal introduction.

Christie Owen & Davies plc v King (1998)

This is a Scottish case heard in the Court of Session. The agent incorporated the Scottish version of the statutory explanation of the sole selling rights. This is the same as the English with the substitution of the words 'missives ... concluded' for 'contracts ... exchanged' in accordance with the Scottish practice of conveyancing. The relevant clause in the contract of agency was:

> '… if unconditional missives for the sale of the property are concluded after the expiry of the period during which we have sole selling rights but to a purchaser who was introduced to you during that period or with whom we had negotiations about the property during that period.'

The vendor (defender) placed a nursing home in the hands of the agent (pursuer) on sole selling rights terms in accordance with the statutory explanation. After nine months, the vendor terminated the contract of agency. He then sold the nursing home to a company run by two men, both of whom had received details of the home from the agent. One of the men had telephoned the vendor soon after he had terminated the agency contract to ask if the property was still on the market. The vendor had not previously known of this man's existence. The agent claimed commission for the sale.

One of the issues in the case was whether the eventual purchaser had been 'introduced to you' during the period of the agency contract. The vendor claimed no such introduction was made. The Court of Session dismissed this pedantic approach. The Court observed that the cases (on effective cause) had clearly established that actual introduction of the purchaser to the seller is not necessary. The important thing is that the parties were put together in a business relationship. It was therefore held that a purchaser is within the clause:

> '… if it is established that he was introduced to the property or brought into a relationship with it through the actings of the agent. We do not consider that any personal introduction to the defender is required.'

The Court observed that, if they were to hold otherwise, an unscrupulous vendor could take unfair advantage where a potential purchaser, having been sent details by the agent, contacts the vendor directly. In such a case, the vendor could terminate the agency then complete the sale. 'The commercial purpose of a clause of this type is to take account of such a temptation and the consequent need for vigilance on the part of the agents.'

Sale of property

The statutory definitions of sole selling rights and sole agency use the words 'sale' and 'purchaser'. Unless the contract of agency also includes terms covering a transaction which is not a 'sale' of property, such as the grant of a lease at a rack rent, the agent risks losing commission if the client enters into such a transaction.

Dowling Kerr Ltd v Scott (1996)

The plaintiff agents entered into an agreement with the defendant to sell his business. The agreement contemplated a sale of the freehold or the grant of a 21-year lease at a premium.

The commission was to be due when 'either a sale is made to a purchaser under the terms of this Sole Selling Rights Agreement or a ready, willing and able purchaser is found'.

The amount of commission was calculated on the eventual 'sale price' of the business (however apportioned between goodwill, fixtures and fittings) leasehold or freehold, at 4.5 per cent for the freehold, and 6 per cent for leaseholds plus 10 per cent of the passing annual rent. The minimum fee was £3,000. No fees were to be charged on value of stock. The agency agreement granted the plaintiffs sole selling rights so, in accordance with the regulations, the statutory explanation was included in the contract. The agreement was for six months and continued thereafter until terminated by either side on 14 days' notice. During the continuation of the agreement, the defendant granted a 12-year lease of the property at an annual rent of £11,400 with no premium. Fixtures and fittings were sold for £1,300. Stock was sold for £1,700. When the plaintiffs found out about the lease, they claimed the minimum commission of £3,000.

The Court of Appeal held that there was 'no sale of the property for either of the interests which the contract evidently contemplated'. Therefore no commission was due.

4.5.2 **Damages for client's breach of sole agency and sole selling rights agreements**

Where the client instructs another agent during the period of sole agency, he commits a breach of contract. Likewise, a client who has entered a sole selling rights agreement is in breach of contract if he undertakes a private sale. The amount of damages is based on the loss of the opportunity of earning commission. The proportion this bears to the amount of commission depends on the facts and circumstances of the case. In an appropriate case, the full commission may be awarded.

Hampton & Sons v George (1939)

The lessee of a hotel was seeking a buyer for his lease. He instructed the plaintiffs as sole agents and thereby terminated the authority of an agent he had previously instructed. The purchaser had previously put in an offer through the previous agents, but this had been rejected. After the sole agency agreement was entered into, the purchaser put the same offer through the previous agents again, and this time the offer was accepted. The plaintiffs claimed commission or, in the alternative, damages. The judge found that the commission for introducing the purchaser would have been £104. In assessing damages, the judge considered the chances of the plaintiffs finding another buyer, as he considered that they would have difficulty in proving that they were the effective cause of the introduction of the actual buyer if she had been referred to them by the lessee (as he should have done). Matters he took into account included the fact that Hamptons, although experienced and efficient, were not specialists in the licensed trade, and the brewers were not easily satisfied with a prospective buyer. He also considered the possibility that the plaintiffs might have got more out of the actual buyer or another potential buyer, and whether they might have found a buyer within a reasonable time so that the lessee would not have determined their agency.

The plaintiffs were awarded £80, slightly more than three-quarters of the commission.

Gross Fine & Krieger Chalfen v Gaynor (1975)

The plaintiffs were instructed to auction the defendant's property. As usual in auction agreements, the plaintiffs were made sole agents. Because of the intervention of the defendant's daughter and a failure to grasp the nature of business procedures, another agent was instructed to find a buyer by private treaty. Such a buyer was found and the property sold for £61,000 before any auction could take place. The plaintiffs claimed their commission based on the purchase price obtained plus expenses. In awarding full commission, the judge stated that the market was buoyant and observed that later in the same year the property was resold for over £70,000. Furthermore, he found that a substantial measurements error in the preliminary auction particulars would have been corrected by the time of the auction or made no difference to the price obtained.

Property Choice v Fronda (1991)

The plaintiff agents entered into a sole selling rights agreement with the defendant vendors. The defendants accepted an offer, subject to contract, from a private buyer. This was a breach of contract and the county court judge assessed damages at 20 per cent less than the full commission. The defendants appealed on a different issue and won. However, had the quantum of damages arisen before the Court of Appeal, Lord Justice Nichols stated that there would have been a 'very modest award'. This is because the county court judge had not taken account of the reason that the private sale was never concluded, i.e. the defendants becoming unwilling to sell, resulting in the buyer having to give up and look elsewhere. There was no reason to believe that the result would have been any different in respect of the buyer that had been introduced by Property Choice.

Michael Harwood t/a RSBS Group v Smith (1998)

It was held that an agent with sole selling rights is not entitled to commission where the buyer is introduced by another agent during the sole selling rights agreement, provided that contracts are exchanged after the agreement has come to an end. However, Lord Justice Pill observed in passing that the point at issue in the case could be academic because the damage, which flowed from the breach, 'was in the commission which Mr Harwood would have earned had [the defendants] referred the prospective purchaser to him as the agent with sole selling rights'. Unfortunately, the Court was not called upon to make a finding on this point.

4.5.3 Provisions for remuneration in the event of sale through another

A sole agency or sole selling agreement may provide that, in the event of a purchaser being introduced by another agent or the client entering into a private sale, commission will be due. It is arguable that such a provision is not really a commission clause, but a provision as to damages for breach of contract. If so, it must be a genuine pre-estimate of the likely loss, otherwise it is a penalty clause and therefore unenforceable. However, the statutory explanations of sole agency and sole selling rights (above) provide that commission is payable in such cases, so they have the seal of legislative approval

Although the remuneration provisions in the statutory explanations are not penalties, this does not preclude other provisions disguised as commission clauses being construed as such.

Chris Hart (Business Sales) Ltd v Mitchell (1996)

Sole agents were engaged to find a buyer for the vendors' hotel. During the term of the agency the agents failed to find a buyer, so the vendors terminated the agency, advertised the business and subsequently found a buyer themselves. The agents claimed commission on two grounds. First, that the contract provided for commission if they had 'contributed in any way to that sale'. The agents claimed that as the vendors had based their advertisement on the agents' particulars of sale, they had contributed to the sale. The Court found no evidence to show how far this had contributed to the actual sale, if at all; it was not sufficient to contribute in some way to the selling process.

The second ground was based on a clause in the contract which required the vendors to submit any offer to purchase to the agents before sending it to their solicitors. This applied even after the agency contract was terminated. The purpose of this was to enable the agents to assess what contribution they had made to a sale so as to justify a claim for remuneration. In the event of failure to submit any such offer to the agents, their whole remuneration and outlays would be payable (nearly £7,500). So the agents claimed they were entitled to payment.

The sheriff principal rejected the agent's claim that the clause in question was a provision entirely separate from the matter of damages. On the contrary, it was 'nothing more or less than a stipulation relating to damages'. And as it was not a genuine pre-estimate of the loss the agents would suffer if they were not informed of the sale, it was a penalty and so unenforceable.

[**Note:** As to penalties, price escalation clauses and other unfair contract terms, see below under consumer protection at 5.5.]

A clause which provides for the consequences of a breach may inadvertently exclude the agent's usual right to claim damages, for if nothing is recoverable under the terms of the all-encompassing clause, the agent is without a remedy.

Property Choice v Fronda (1991)

A sole selling rights agreement provided that, until the expiry of the agreement, 'the vendor will not consent to sell the property to anyone not introduced by the agents'. It continued: 'If this is contravened [the agents] will be entitled to the same commission in the same circumstances as if we had effected an introduction.' The county court judge found the latter clause to be an unenforceable penalty. He therefore awarded damages for breach in respect of the acceptance by the vendors of an offer, subject to contract, from a private buyer. On appeal by the vendors, the Court of Appeal observed that the clause requires the Court to determine whether the agents would have been entitled to commission had they, rather than the vendors, introduced the private buyer. As the vendors backed out of the deal with the private buyer, there would have been no entitlement to commission. And as the clause set out what is to be the remedy in the event of the breach, it precluded a claim for damages.

Unfortunately, the Court did not have to determine whether the clause was a penalty or not.

4.6 ENTRY INTO COMMISSION AGREEMENTS

As in any contract, an offeror cannot deem that the offeree has accepted his proposals if he does not hear from him to the contrary (*Felthouse v Bindley*). Mere silence is not acceptance. Furthermore, in the case of an oral agreement, confirming letters must accurately reflect that agreement, and new terms cannot be incorporated without further agreement. However, if a confirming letter is sent and the client continues to instruct the agent, at common law this may be taken by the court to indicate that the confirming letter actually represents the contract. (See 4.6.1 below for the effect of *Estate Agents Act 1979*, section 18 on this practice now.)

Way & Waller v Ryde (1944)

The plaintiffs agreed to find a purchaser for the defendant's hotel. The plaintiffs wrote to the defendant enclosing a scale of remuneration. Even though this was higher than the usual or recognised scale, the Court of Appeal held that the defendant was bound by its terms.

> 'With the letter before him he allowed them to continue. He allowed them to do work ... He agreed to it by conduct for better or worse, and whatever it is, be it high or low, he is bound by it, in my opinion.' (Lord Greene MR)

John E Trinder & Partners v Haggis (1951)

A representative of the plaintiff agents called at the defendant's house and spoke to his wife. Nothing was said at the meeting as to any commission payable to the plaintiffs.

On the same day, the plaintiffs wrote a confirming letter stating the commission payable in the event of their introducing a person willing to sign a contract. A few months later, the plaintiffs found a buyer willing to pay a sum lower than the asking price. The defendant authorised the plaintiffs to agree to sell at that figure.

The Court of Appeal held, Lord Justice Denning dissenting, that the defendant had by his conduct, which could not in the circumstances by referable to any other terms of engagement, bound himself in the terms of the plaintiffs' letter.

Agent introduces a tenant who subsequently purchases

Where the agent is instructed to find a tenant and does so, the courts have traditionally taken the view that the agent's employment is thereby terminated, and no commission is due if the tenant subsequently purchases the property. Even if the agent can establish that he is the effective cause of the sale, he is not entitled to commission unless he can show that he has a continuous retainer or contract to find a buyer. Thus if the principal does not expressly agree to pay commission if the tenant subsequently purchases, it may be difficult for the agent to show that there is such a contract by conduct. The existence of a confirming letter will be insufficient evidence without conduct which is referable to a contract to find a buyer and not just a tenant.

Toulmin v Millar (1887)

In 1880 Toulmin, the tenant for life of a settled estate, engaged Millar to let the property. Millar gave Toulmin a scale of charges for both selling and leasing which contained a note that when property was let to a tenant who afterwards became the purchaser, the commission on selling would be charged, less the amount of commission on letting. Toulmin put the paper in his pocket without reading it. Millar introduced a person who took a lease to see how he liked it. Then the *Settled Land Act* 1882 was passed. This gave a tenant for life the power to sell. So Toulmin sold the property to the tenant for £70,000 without the intervention of Millar.

The House of Lords held that the agent was simply employed to let and so was not entitled to commission on the subsequent sale.

In the world of non-retained agents, there may be uncertainty about the terms of any contract. The question of whether there is a commission contract at all and, if so, the terms of remuneration, is a question of fact. The mere existence of a 'confirming letter' routinely sent out by an estate agent will not, of itself, be sufficient evidence of a contract. But when linked with other material, such as evidence of conduct and oral testimony, it may at least be evidence of the amount of remuneration where a contract is established.

4.6.1 Written details of charges, etc – Estate Agents Act 1979, section 18

This section, together with the *Estate Agents (Provision of Information) Regulations* 1991, requires the estate agent to notify the client in writing of details of any charges that may become due. This includes any payments, such as advertising expenses, that are payable to the agent or another person.

The information to be given is set out in section 18(2) as follows:

(a) particulars of the circumstances in which the client will become liable to pay remuneration to the agent for carrying out estate agency work;

(b) particulars of the amount of the agent's remuneration for carrying out estate agency work or, if that amount is not ascertainable at the time the information is given, particulars of the manner in which the remuneration will be calculated;

(c) particulars of any payments which do not form part of the agent's remuneration for carrying out estate agency work or a contract or pre-contract deposit but which, under the contract referred to in subsection (1) above, will or may in certain circumstances be payable by the client to the agent or any other person and particulars of the circumstances in which any such payments will become payable; and

(d) particulars of the amount of any payment falling within paragraph (c) above or, if that amount is not ascertainable at the time the information is given, an estimate of that amount together with particulars of the manner in which it will be calculated.

The notice of charges must be provided **before** the contract is entered into with the client. Failure to comply with section 18 renders the contract unenforceable without leave of court, regardless of whether there would be a binding contract at common law. Therefore, if a letter containing details of the fees of the agent is claimed to be a 'confirming letter', it will be too late to comply with section 18. However, a letter complying with section 18 may constitute an offer, which may be taken to be accepted by evidence of the conduct of the client.

Day Morris Associates v Voyce (2003)

The plaintiffs claimed that the defendant had instructed them to market her house and that she had entered into a commission agreement with them. The defendant denied entering any agreement. She had signed no contract, and claimed that her interest in selling the property was tentative. A letter had been sent by the plaintiffs which confirmed and thanked the defendant for her instructions and provided information about charges. It was obviously designed to comply with the requirements of section 18 and the Court of Appeal stated that it 'could only therefore be a pre-contract document'. The plaintiffs asked the defendant to return a signed copy of the letter and to fill in an enclosed questionnaire so that they could prepare the property particulars. The defendant did not respond, and claimed that she treated the letter almost as 'junk mail'. The issue for the Court was whether the conduct of the defendant after receipt of the letter amounted to acceptance of its terms. She allowed the plaintiffs to produce particulars of the property which were given to prospective purchasers and to advertise it by showing people round. (She had handed over the keys before the offer letter had been written, and had not asked to retrieve them.) Such acquiescence in the marketing of the property could signify acceptance and, on the background of the dealings between the parties, it did. Therefore commission was due when the plaintiffs introduced a person who eventually purchased the property.

[**Note:** This remained the case even though, in divorce proceedings, she subsequently ceded authority to her husband, the joint owner, to sell the house.]

In the event of failure to comply with section 18, the estate agent may apply to the Court for enforcement. The Court will dismiss the application if it is just to do so having regard to the prejudice to the client. If the Court does not dismiss the application, it may reduce the commission to compensate the client for any prejudice suffered.

Solicitors' Estate Agency (Glasgow) Ltd v MacIver (1993)

The agent received an 18 per cent discount for a block advertisement in the *Glasgow Herald*. This discount was not revealed to the client and the full charge was passed on. When the agents sought their fees and advertising costs, the client claimed the contract was unenforceable because the particulars of an amount of non-remuneration payment had not been provided, contrary to section 18(2)(d), above.

The sheriff described the conduct of the agents as 'significantly culpable' because it not only deprived the vendor of the discount, but also deprived him of information which might have led him to consider his position more carefully and perhaps seek a quotation elsewhere. He determined that the contract should be enforced, but awarded a reduction of 50 per cent (£317) of the sum due to compensate the vendor for the prejudice suffered.

On appeal to the sheriff principal, it was held that the agents were also in breach of section 18(2)(a) because, in effect, the secret discount was undisclosed remuneration. The sheriff principal therefore held that the sheriff's exercise of discretion was vitiated, and determined that the entire contract was unenforceable because a breach of paragraphs

(a) and (b) was more serious than a breach of paragraphs (c) and (d), as the former relate to remuneration. However, the Court of Session restored the sheriff's original decision because the breach of paragraph (a) had not been argued before him. Furthermore, he had considered all material factors and had clearly understood that the client was being overcharged.

Variation of terms

Section 18 also requires the agent to provide details in writing of any agreed variation.

Fiesta Girl of London Ltd v Network Agencies (1992)

The agent noted an agreed variation in his commission charges on the back of a business card and signed it. Although what he wrote did not clearly accord with the actual variation orally agreed with the client, the agent was held not to be in breach of section 18 because, at the time the event occurred, the *Estate Agents (Provision of Information) Regulations* 1991 had not come into effect and it was not necessary to put the information required by section 18 in writing. Today, of course, the agent would be in breach.

4.6.2 Cold calling

A commission contract must comply with the normal legal rules of contract formation. The provision of an unrequested benefit, such as information about a possible buyer or seller, does not, of itself, create a contract. It is past consideration. But a clearly expressed undertaking to provide further information, even if of little value, will constitute an offer which may be accepted by the recipient by, for example, seeking that information from the offeror.

Lady Manor Ltd v Fat Cat Café Bars Ltd (2001)

The claimant estate agent sent a letter to the defendant containing unrequested information about a property. The letter also stated what fee would become payable if the introduction led to a successful transaction. The defendant subsequently purchased the property. The claimant sought commission. The Court held that there was no contract and the information provided could be used without obligation. Only if further information is to be provided is proper consideration given. This further information may be of little value, such as the identity of the vendor's agent in order to arrange a viewing. The claimant claimed that the information about the vendor's agent was such further information, so a contract had been made. Unfortunately for the claimant in this case, the letter was not clearly expressed as an offer to provide further information for a fee. It wrongly suggested that the introduction was given pursuant to an agreement that a fee would be paid. There was no such agreement. It used the expressions 'as discussed' and 'confirm' when there had been no previous communication whatsoever. On the facts, the judge found that the letter was not sufficiently clear, and no agreement was made.

4.6.3 Fulfilment of instructions

Commission is only due for fulfilment of instructions. However, where the agent has not performed the instructions to the letter but he has, in substance, achieved what the client is seeking, he may still be entitled to commission, depending upon the circumstances. Each case turns on its own facts and on the terms of the agency contract. If the agent achieves something materially different from the instructions, he will usually fail to obtain commission – the courts will not imply a term for payment of commission unless it is necessary to give the contract business efficacy. But it is dangerous to generalise and wrong to regard each case as a precedent.

The lesson for agents is to draft their agreements widely enough to cover a similar event or a similar way of achieving the same result. For example, an underlease as well as a lease (see *Richard Ellis v Pipe-Chem (Holdings) Ltd*, below).

Rimmer v Knowles (1874)

The plaintiff agent was instructed to find a purchaser of the defendant's land. He introduced a buyer who offered £2,600, but the defendant wanted £3,000. The deadlock was resolved by an agreement granting the buyer a 999-year lease at a rent of five per cent of the sum required by the defendant (£150 p.a.) with an option to purchase in the first 20 years. This was held to be a sale in the ordinary sense of the word, though not in the legal sense, because it enabled the buyer to pay the £3,000 'by degrees' as it was coupled with an option to purchase. The judges were unanimous in finding that the plaintiff substantially performed his agreement and so was entitled to his commission.

Griffin & Son v Cheesewright (1885)

The defendant had a long lease of a house. He instructed Griffin Senior of the plaintiff agents to sublet it for three years at a rent of £75 p.a. The plaintiffs introduced a prospective tenant to view the house. Her father went to see the house and found a card showing that the defendant was the owner. He then bought the 75-year residue of the house from the defendant for £1,100. The defendant only paid the commission to which the plaintiffs were entitled if they had found a tenant to take a three-year lease. The plaintiffs claimed commission on sale but were found not entitled to it. The plaintiffs had based their claim on express authority, given to Griffin Junior, to sell the long lease, but on the facts no such authority was found. The possibility of implied authority was, unfortunately, not pleaded. In any case, it appears that the contract of sale had not been proved to have been brought about by the plaintiffs.

Richard Ellis v Pipe-Chem (Holdings) Ltd (1980)

The plaintiff agents were engaged to find premises for the defendant company. The plaintiffs found suitable premises and it was agreed that commission would be due 'when the lease has been completed'. The landlord was not satisfied with the financial position of the defendant, and so the defendant suggested that another company (a creditor of the defendant) be granted a lease identical to the one sought by the defendants, which would then be underleased to the defendant on similar terms. When these transactions were completed, the plaintiffs claimed commission.

The judge found that there was no deliberate intention to create a device to avoid payment. Therefore commission was not due as the commission earning event – the lease to the defendant – had not occurred. There was no justification to imply a term giving the plaintiffs' commission. It was not necessary in order to give the contract business efficacy.

Dowling Kerr Ltd v Scott (1996)

The plaintiff agents entered into an agreement with the defendant to sell his business. The agreement contemplated a sale of the freehold or the grant of a 21-year lease at a premium. Eventually the defendant granted a 12-year lease with no premium. The Court of Appeal held that there was 'no sale of the property for either of the interests which the contract evidently contemplated'. Therefore no commission was due.

Levers v Dunsdon (1967)

The agent took instructions to find a purchaser of the defendants' garage business, including freehold property, fixtures, fittings and equipment. It was agreed that if the agent got a price of £85,000, anything over that would be the commission. The agent introduced a purchaser who eventually purchased the business, not by buying the assets of the business but by buying the defendants' shares and thus acquiring the company. In the view of the judge, the commission agreement was wide enough to cover the sale of shares, at least in the case where the price of shares was calculated as it was.

Where a company's property is subject to a mortgage, the value of the shares is normally depressed by the mortgage liability. Where land is sold, however, it is not the equity in the house that determines the price. Instead, the mortgage is disregarded as it will normally be discharged on sale. The difference in price obtained will obviously affect the amount of commission earned on a percentage basis, unless provided for in the commission agreement. In the *Levers* case, however, the sale agreement provided for a price of £85,000 'less all current liabilities ... except the mortgage ...'. Therefore, the share buyers had agreed to purchase the company, subject to the mortgage, but with no allowance on account of the mortgage. So the amount required to secure the mortgage (£5,890) was, in effect, added to the purchase price, earning the agent commission of exactly that amount.

Whether a mortgage is disregarded on a sale of shares depends on the facts.

Way & Waller v Ryde (1944)

The defendant owned all the shares but one in a limited company, the assets of which comprised a hotel. The hotel was mortgaged for £15,000 and the share capital in the company was £10,000. Having found a purchaser, the plaintiffs claimed commission as a percentage of £25,000, the value of the hotel. However, the purchaser had bought the company at a price of £10,000 so the Court of Appeal awarded commission on that basis.

Although the parties may have loosely used the phrase 'selling the hotel', there was nothing in the contract to support the agents' claim that they be paid for something they never effected, namely, a sale of the hotel subject to a mortgage. The actual transaction was a sale of the shares.

4.7 FORFEITURE OF COMMISSION

In the normal course of events, the agent who achieves the result bargained for will obtain his commission. However, the law of agency attaches great significance to the duty of loyalty (above) so, even though the commission event has occurred, the agent may forfeit his right to commission. Furthermore, consistent with the law of contract, an agent who breaches an essential term of the contract may lose the right to commission.

4.7.1 **Forfeiture for breach of duty of loyalty**

Having an undisclosed interest in the transaction and acting for both sides are common examples of breach of loyalty disentitling the agent to commission.

Salomons v Pender (1865)

The plaintiff agent introduced a purchaser which was a company in which the agent had a substantial shareholding. Commission was forfeited.

Andrew v Ramsay & Co (1903)

The defendant estate agents introduced a purchaser who paid the defendant commission for the transaction. Commission was forfeited.

Fullwood v Hurley (1928)

The plaintiff agent claimed commission from the defendant for finding a hotel for him to purchase. When the defendant found out that the agent had obtained commission from the vendor of the hotel he refused to pay. It was held that the plaintiff could not act for both vendor and purchaser without the consent of both, therefore no commission was due.

Henry Smith & Son v Muskett (1978)

The plaintiff agents agreed with a prospective purchaser of their client's property that, if the prospective purchaser bought the property, he would retain the agent and pay commission for reletting the property. It was held that this agreement disentitled the agent to commission.

Breach of the duty of loyalty does not automatically result in the forfeiture of commission. Depending on the gravity of the breach of duty, the Court may award an agent his commission, subject to a claim in damages, if the agent acted honestly and in good faith.

Keppel v Wheeler (1927)

Having found a buyer subject to contract, the agent passed on another offer, not to the vendor, but to the buyer. On the facts it was found that the agent honestly believed he had discharged his duties to the vendor by finding a buyer subject to contract, so commission was due. However, the agent was liable in damages for breach of contract in not passing on the offer to the vendor.

Robinson Scammell & Co v Ansell (1985)

The vendors' agent was informed by another agent that the vendors might pull out because the 'chain' above them had collapsed. Having tried and failed to contact the vendor, the agent then telephoned the purchasers to inform them of the situation. The vendors did not in fact pull out and the deal went through. It was held that the agents had committed a breach of duty, but were entitled to their commission because, following *Keppel v Wheeler*, they had acted honestly and in good faith.

4.7.2 Forfeiture of commission for breach of condition

Where a party is in breach of an essential term or condition of the contract, the innocent party is entitled to rescind the contract and claim damages. A term which is not a condition, usually called a warranty or a minor term, only entitles the innocent party to sue for damages. Whether a term of the contract is a condition or a warranty depends upon the intention of the parties as revealed by the construction of the contract in the light of the surrounding circumstances. Informing a prospective purchaser that the client vendor will accept less than the asking price without obtaining his authority beforehand, may be a breach of condition.

Spiers v Taylor (1984)

The terms of the agent's instructions included: 'The property to be advertised without cost to the vendor and entered on the agents list of properties for sale at the asking price of

£34,500'. Without the authority of the client vendor, the agent informed a prospective purchaser that the vendor would accept £33,000. He then wrote to the vendor stating that the prospective purchaser had agreed to purchase the property for the asking price. This was false. Later the vendor discovered that the purchaser had only offered £33,500. The vendor was not prepared to accept this price but eventually agreed with the purchaser on a price of £34,000 and the sale went through. (The vendor wished to avoid breaking the chain of sales.)

The Court of Appeal held that the instruction to advertise at the stipulated asking price was an essential term of the contract. No commission was due until this condition was fulfilled. The vendor was also entitled to damages for loss.

[**Note:** The High Court had fixed damages at £50 for the loss of a chance of obtaining a higher price.]

4.8 AMOUNT OF COMMISSION

Abolition of scale fees

The *Restriction on Agreements (Estate Agents) Order* 1970 (SI 1970/1696), made under section 56 of the *Fair Trading Act* 1973, outlaws price fixing. It is unlawful for two or more estate agents to agree to charge a minimum fee or minimum rate of commission. The legislation prevented sanctions being taken by a professional body against a member who chose not to adhere to scale fees, but did not prohibit the publication of recommended scale fees which most members continued to adhere to. The Monopolies Commission stated that this was contrary to free market competition, so RICS abolished scale fees in 1982. Some of the cases set out below were decided in the context of professional scale fees. Today, with no scale to refer to, the courts will have regard to fees commonly charged for the relevant work in the locality where there is a dispute as to the appropriate fee. Fee guidance is now regarded as an unfair trade practice by the Office of Fair Trading.

Quantum meruit – as much as he has earned

It has been clearly established since *Luxor v Cooper* that where an agent is to be paid commission to achieve a result, he gets paid only when he achieves that result. He therefore has no claim on a quantum meruit basis for the work done in introducing a prospective purchaser if the vendor decides not to proceed with the purchase; unless of course that introduction actually is the achievement of the result required, such as introduction of a ready, willing and able purchaser (above). But a claim in quantum meruit may be sustainable where the agent has fulfilled his instructions but there is no clear agreement as to commission, or there is no agreement as to the payment of any fee at all. In the former, the court will usually determine a reasonable remuneration which may amount to the full commission if the agreement is for remuneration on a commission basis. In the latter situation there is arguably no contract at all, but the employment of a person in a professional capacity raises a rebuttable presumption that he is to be paid for his services, so a contract is implied and remuneration will be on a quantum meruit basis, i.e. as much as he has earned. Also, where a contract is unenforceable, the agent may be able to claim quantum meruit.

As the cases below show, it is vital for agents to ensure that their terms of commission have been agreed before embarking on agency work, because the court's award will be less than a claimed percentage of the sale price if remuneration is calculated on an hourly rate for work done. In any event, section 18 of the *Estate Agents Act* 1979 requires details about the charges in respect of estate agency work to be provided before the contract is entered into, so disputes about the amount of commission should now be rare.

Lewis & Graves v Harper (1979)

The defendant instructed the plaintiff agents to sell his house. There was no understanding as to the rate of commission, but it was understood that the basis of remuneration should be by way of commission. After the sale was completed, the agents sent a bill to the defendant for £286 based on the old scales laid down in the *Estates Gazette*. When this was challenged, the plaintiffs stated that it was the going rate but offered to reduce it by ten pounds. The defendant claimed that a fair and reasonable sum would not exceed £100. As there was an agreement for payment by commission, quantum meruit was not in issue. Therefore, it was for the court to determine what a reasonable commission would be in the circumstances of the case. The county court judge awarded the £276 claimed, and the Court of Appeal found no reason to disagree.

Withey Robinson v Edwards (1986)

The plaintiffs were instructed by the defendant who was intending to purchase a night club. They were to provide valuations, prepare an inventory of fixtures and fittings, take details of trading figures and generally assist the defendant in negotiations with the prospective vendor (with whom the defendant had already had discussions). After the purchase was completed, the plaintiffs claimed the sum of £5,980 based on the former RICS scale. It was found that there was no express or implied term that remuneration should be on the RICS scale, so the plaintiffs were awarded a sum on a quantum meruit basis. The county court judge calculated that they were entitled to £80 per hour for 45 hours plus VAT – a total of £4,140. This was upheld in the Court of Appeal.

Chaskill Ltd v Marina Developments Ltd (1988)

The plaintiffs claimed £15,000 commission for introducing the defendants to a company developing a marina. No specific fee had been agreed, so the judge awarded 'reasonable fees' for the introduction (it was not based on quantum meruit). In determining the fees, the judge did not accept that the plaintiffs should be compensated for the commercial opportunity they afforded to the defendants. Instead, he valued the claim on the basis of time properly spent in effecting the introduction. On the evidence the plaintiffs had spent 8.5 hours on the matter and he awarded them £150 per hour, bearing in mind the nature and complexity of the work. Nothing was awarded in respect of work done after the introduction had been effected, as the contract was confined to introducing the defendants. Nothing was awarded for any preparatory work carried out by the plaintiffs in informing themselves in order that they were properly equipped to interest the defendants, for that was nothing to do with the defendants. The total came to £2,325.

Debenham Tewson & Chinnocks plc v Rimington (1989)

The plaintiffs had carried out the defendant vendor's instructions to discuss values with the purchaser's agent, but had not, on the facts, carried out negotiations for sale of land within the terms of the commission agreement. (The principals agreed the price themselves.) Therefore, they were awarded £15,000 on a quantum meruit basis, rather than the 1.5 per cent commission on the £32.5m purchase price that they claimed.

Bentall, Horsley and Baldry v Vicary (1931)

The plaintiffs were engaged by the defendant as sole agents. The defendant found a purchaser himself. It was held that the plaintiffs were not entitled to commission, nor were they entitled to anything by way of quantum meruit, as they had not introduced the purchaser.

Valuation fees

An agent who intends to charge for a valuation if no purchaser is found, must include clear terms to that effect in the contract.

Gross Fine & Krieger Chalfen v Clifton (1974)

The defendant agent was instructed to sell property in London. Needing a valuation of the commercial part, he employed a chartered surveyor of the plaintiff company to provide one and indicated that the usual scale fee would be paid on sale. The surveyor wrote to the defendant saying:

'... it would not be unreasonable to look to you for a valuation fee in the event of our not receiving commission on the usual scale in the event of our selling this property, and your comments would be appreciated'.

This received an evasive reply and comforting words about the certainty of a sale commission.

The surveyor prepared a valuation of £260,000 and recommended a quotation figure of £325,000. Having already received offers in the region of £350,000, the vendor described the valuation as a 'load of rubbish'. He terminated his business with the defendant and, in a strongly rising market, sold the property 18 months later for £600,000. Having received no sale commission, the defendant refused to pay the plaintiffs' demand for £750 scale fees. The plaintiffs sued for payment.

The plaintiffs contended that there was a contract under which the valuation fees were to be paid in any event, but the judge found there was no such contract. However, he found that there was an implied obligation to pay for services rendered so he had to determine the reasonable remuneration. He determined that scale fees could only be charged in appropriate circumstances, and was of the opinion that the valuation did not of itself attract a scale fee nor had it the intrinsic merit to justify the full scale. However, he rejected the claim that the valuation was negligent and found the true value to be half way between the two opposing views, i.e. half the scale fee.

4.9 COSTS AND EXPENSES

It has been established that an estate agent is normally paid for a result, not for services, and therefore will not be entitled to recover costs and expenses incurred without express agreement. Furthermore, section 18 of the *Estate Agents Act* 1979 requires particulars of payments to be provided before the contract is entered into. This information must now be in writing – *Estate Agents (Provision of Information) Regulations* 1991.

4.9.1 **Indemnity for tortious acts**

Generally speaking, a principal and agent are jointly and severally liable for the torts of the agent acting within his authority. Therefore, an injured party may choose to sue either. If so, the *Civil Liability (Contribution) Act* 1978 allows the person sued to recover contribution from the other, the proportion of the contribution depending on responsibility.

A person wholly to blame cannot recover anything from the innocent party. Furthermore, at common law the innocent party, whether agent or principal, is entitled to an indemnity from the wrongdoer.

Adamson v Jarvis (1827)

The principal represented to an auctioneer that he was the owner of cattle and other goods and purported to authorise the auctioneer to sell them. The auctioneer was unaware of the fact that the principal had no right to sell the goods. After the sale, the true owner sued the auctioneer in the tort of conversion and was awarded damages of £1,195. The auctioneer also incurred costs of £500 in defending himself. The auctioneer sought an indemnity from the principal. The Court held that, so long as the party seeking the indemnity is innocent and is not aware of the unlawfulness of the act, he is entitled to be indemnified by the wrongdoer in respect of his losses.

5

Consumer protection and related laws

5.1 PROPERTY MISDESCRIPTIONS ACT 1991

False or misleading statements in the course of estate agency business

The *Property Misdescriptions Act* 1991 ('the 1991 Act') creates the criminal offence of making any 'false or misleading statement … in the course of an estate agency business or a property development business, otherwise than in providing conveyancing services'.

Enforcement is the responsibility of trading standards departments of local authorities. The 1991 Act is based on the *Trade Descriptions Act* 1972 and uses much the same terminology. The cases on that Act are therefore of relevance in the interpretation of the provisions in the 1991 Act.

A statement is made 'in the course of an estate agency business' if it would constitute 'estate agency work' within the definition in section 1(1) of the *Estate Agents Act* 1979. Essentially this covers things done, pursuant to instructions from a person who wishes to buy or sell an interest in land, with a view to effecting an introduction of a prospective buyer or seller, and for securing the transaction. Property development business is defined as a business concerned wholly or substantially with the development of land.

There is no duty to disclose information, but if information is disclosed it must be true. See Chapter 3 as to the meaning of misrepresentation.

'False' is defined as 'false to a material degree'. A statement is 'misleading' if (though not false) what a reasonable person may be expected to infer from it, or from any omission from it, is 'false'. Thus a half truth may be a false statement. Each time that a false statement is made, a separate offence is committed. Therefore distribution of property particulars containing one mistake may lead to the commission of a series of offences.

A 'statement' may be made by pictures or any other method of signifying meaning as well as by words. If made by words, it may be made orally or in writing. Examples already exist in civil law of misrepresentations as to property being made by conduct and other means. See the cases in Chapter 3.

Offence

Where a false or misleading statement is made in the course of an estate agency or property development business, the person who carries on the business is guilty of an offence. Where the statement is due to the act or default of an employee, the employee may be proceeded against whether or not proceedings are taken against the employer. Where the business is carried on by a company, any director, manager, secretary or other similar officer who has contributed to the commission of the offence by connivance or consent is also guilty of an offence.

Prescribed matters

The 1991 Act applies only in respect of statements made about prescribed matters. These are to be found in the *Property Misdescriptions (Specified Matters) Order* 1992. It contains a comprehensive list of 33 matters including construction, tenure, condition, view, location, price, planning, services, compliance with regulations, easements, and many other factual matters.

Disclaimers

Whilst it is not possible to exclude liability by a general disclaimer, it may be possible to neutralise the effect of a false description or contradict its effect by clear words. However, the Court of Appeal held in *Norman v Bennett*, a case on the *Trade Descriptions Act* 1972, that in order for a disclaimer to have that effect it must be 'as bold, precise and compelling as the trade description itself'. So a statement in the small print: 'speedometer reading not guaranteed' did not satisfy that test. The disclaimer must equal the description in effect. (For example, a notice on the speedometer itself.) It is likely that this approach will be taken to cases under the 1991 Act.

Statements of opinion

Although an opinion may be false, if it is honestly believed it is not a false statement of fact. Therefore an honest statement of opinion is not in breach of the 1991 Act, so long as it really is a matter of opinion and not of fact. Matters of taste are matters of opinion. But statements such as 'highly desirable location' are matters of fact, and cannot be turned into opinion by a clause in the particulars which states that 'all statements herein are matters of opinion only' or similar words. See Chapter 3 for a fuller explanation and for cases on this in civil law.

Promises

A promise or prediction may come true. If it does not, that in itself does not make the promise a false statement. However, a maker of a promise is implying that his present intention is to keep the promise or that he has the power to perform it. If that is not the case, he is making a false statement as to an existing fact – his present intention.

Lewin v Barratt Homes Ltd (2000)

Barratt Homes were prosecuted under the 1991 Act for misleading prospective purchasers, in the course of a property development business, about the external design of homes they were building.

At a site office, two purchasers were shown a picture of a house type known as a 'Maidstone' which was being offered for sale. They were also invited to look at, and did visit, a show house of the same design. At this time Barratt knew that, for planning reasons, they could not build houses of this type.

Beneath the picture in the site office there appeared in writing an 'IMPORTANT NOTICE' that pointed out that the visual depictions could not be relied upon as an accurate description. At the bottom of the picture was a sticker which stated in bold capital letters: 'DETAILS OF THIS PROPERTY HAVE BEEN AMENDED. PLEASE REFER TO SITE NEGOTIATOR FOR DETAILS'. On the office wall was a framed A4 document headed 'IMPORTANT NOTICE' that warned that there might be a difference between the accommodation depicted in Barratt's literature and that on offer in particular developments. The complainant did not recall anything being brought to his attention which would indicate that the property being built for him would in any way be different from the display pictures or the show house. The houses that were eventually built for the purchasers were of a different external design, so the purchasers complained to the trading standards office. Barratt claimed that there was no misdescription because of the effect of various notices in the site office. This defence failed on the facts, but the magistrates dismissed the charges on the ground that Barratt's information amounted to promises as to the future and not statements of existing fact. The trading standards officer appealed.

The divisional court held that the magistrates were wrong:

> 'It seems quite obvious that by showing prospective purchasers pictures of a Maidstone design and the show house itself, the respondent was stating that that was how it proposed to build the houses. That, in other words, was its present intention ...'

Defence of due diligence

Section 2(1) of the 1991 Act provides that it is a defence for the accused to show that he took all reasonable steps and exercised all due diligence to avoid committing the offence.

Where the accused relied on information provided by another person, the accused must prove that such reliance was reasonable in the circumstances, having regard in particular:

(a) to the steps which he took, and those which might reasonably have been taken, for the purpose of verifying the information; and

(b) to whether he had any reason to disbelieve the information.

The setting up of an effective control system with staff training, records, guidance, etc. may establish the statutory defence of due diligence. Whether the defence is proven is a question of fact in the circumstances of the case.

Enfield London Borough Council v Castles Estate Agents Ltd (1996)

The defendants were employed to market a property. This consisted of a four-bedroomed semi-detached house with a separate single-storey building, which had been built within the curtilage of the main building. The single-storey building had windows, a front door and a porch, and was laid out as a one-bedroomed bungalow. It was set within its own grounds with a low wall dividing it from the main dwelling and the road. A driveway led from the road. A senior negotiator of the defendants inspected the property and asked the vendors if planning permission had been granted for the 'bungalow'. He was told that it had, and so he entered 'perm dev' on his instruction sheet. In fact the building had no planning permission to be used as a one-bedroom bungalow. Subsequently the negotiator sent the property particulars, which referred to a one-bedroom bungalow, to the vendors, together with a Certificate of Confirmation, asking them to sign and return the Certificate verifying the accuracy of the information. They were informed that marketing could not commence until this was done. The vendors never returned the Certificate, despite a telephone reminder. Enfield Borough Council took proceedings against the defendants for describing the building as a bungalow when it could not be used as a dwelling and the magistrates dismissed the case on the ground that the defendants had taken all reasonable steps and exercised all due diligence to avoid committing the offence.

Enfield BC appealed and the Divisional Court held that, on the evidence, the magistrates were entitled to find the statutory defence of due diligence proved. The case concerned a bungalow built 30 or 40 years before which appeared to have been occupied previously, and the Court took the view that it would not be difficult to imagine an experienced agent not even asking the vendor whether it had been built with planning permission. In these circumstances, there would be no steps which would have been reasonable to take to avoid committing the offence and due diligence would have required no further action. It would have been different if the agent had seen 'a newly completed and ugly extension tacked on to the house in a conservation area'. As to the issue of reliance on the vendor's statement, the Court found that the agent thought it prudent to ask and the reply removed any small doubt he might have had. He was not simply relying on what the vendor said, but on his own assessment of the situation supported, to a small extent, by the vendor. If, on the other hand, the agent had real doubt, the vendor's answer would not have been sufficient to rely upon.

5.2   ESTATE AGENTS ACT 1979 – POWERS OF DIRECTOR GENERAL OF FAIR TRADING

The obligations of an estate agent under the *Estate Agents Act* 1979 (the 1979 Act') and regulations made under that Act have been summarised, above. The Act also makes provision for the Office of Fair Trading to prohibit a person from acting as an estate agent or to warn him that, if he continues with a particular practice, he will be prohibited.

Prohibition orders

Under section 3 of the 1979 Act, the Office of Fair Trading (OFT) may prohibit an unfit person from carrying on any estate agency work or estate agency work of a particular description. That power is not exercisable unless one of the triggers, set out below, has occurred. Nevertheless, in determining whether a person is unfit, the OFT may also take account of whether, in the course of estate agency work or any other business activity, that person has engaged in any practice which involves breaches of a duty owed by virtue of any enactment, contract or rule of law and which is material to his fitness to carry on estate agency work.

It is an offence to fail to comply with a prohibition order.

The triggers for action by the OFT are as follows:

(a)　(i) conviction of an offence involving fraud or other dishonesty of violence (see the *Antonelli* case, below),

　　(ii) conviction of an offence under the 1979 Act (with certain exceptions),

　　(iii) conviction of any other offence which, at the time it was committed, was specified by an order made by the Secretary of State;

(b)　discrimination in the course of estate agency work (see below for the definition of discrimination);

(c)　failure to comply with any obligation imposed on him under any of sections 15 and 18 to 21 of the 1979 Act (interest on client's money, provision of information, holding deposits, and disclosure of personal interest);

(d)　engaging in a practice designated as an undesirable practice by order of the Secretary of State.

The *Estate Agents (Undesirable Practices) (No. 2) Order* 1991 declares the following to be undesirable practices within section 3 of the 1979 Act:

(a)　the failure to disclose a personal interest promptly and in writing (includes a beneficial interest in the land of a connected person);

(b)　an act or omission with regard to the provision of services to purchasers (includes discrimination against purchasers not accepting services, as well as failure to provide information promptly and in writing to the client about services provided to a purchaser by the estate agent or a connected person);

(c)　a misdescription or omission of the kind specified in schedule three of the order, namely:

　　(i) knowingly or recklessly making a misrepresentation as to the existence of or details of an offer (see the *Benham* case, below) or as to the existence or status of any prospective purchaser of an interest in the land;

　　(ii) the failure to forward to his client promptly and in writing accurate details (other than those of a description which the client has indicated in writing he does not wish to receive) of any offer the estate agent has received from a prospective purchaser in respect of an interest in the land.

Antonelli v Secretary of State for Trade and Industry (1997)

Antonelli was convicted, in a USA court in 1976, of the offence of setting fire to a property which was not a dwelling house. He subsequently came to the UK from where he carried on business as a property agent. The Director General of Fair Trading considered Antonelli was unfit to engage in estate agency work and disqualified him from undertaking such work on the ground of his conviction. Antonelli appealed to the Secretary of State for Trade and Industry on certain grounds including the following:

- the 1979 Act did not apply to convictions outside the UK;
- the Act did not apply to convictions before the Act came into effect; and
- setting fire to a property which was not a dwelling house was not a crime of violence.

The Secretary of State dismissed the appeal. So Antonelli appealed to the High Court and subsequently to the Court of Appeal. It was held that the Act applied to convictions occurring before the Act was passed and there was no ground for confining the word 'conviction' to conviction of an offence in the UK. All that is required is that the offence has the attributes of dishonesty, fraud or violence. Arson was an act of violence against property, and so the appeal was dismissed. The Court observed that the Director General has wide powers of discretion in determining whether a person is unfit to act as an agent. The conviction itself is not determinative of the imposition of the order of disqualification.

In the context of the *Antonelli* case, it should be noted that section 5(4) of the Act provides that, where the only ground for disqualification is a criminal offence, then the order ceases to have effect as soon as the conviction is spent under the *Rehabilitation of Offenders Act* 1974. However, as the Court observed in *Antonelli*, some offences are so serious that they do not become spent at all.

R v Director General of Fair Trading, ex parte Benhams Ltd (2001)

The applicant estate agents were retained by the vendors of a property. Expressions of interest for sums between £1.1m and £1.2m were received. Contracts were exchanged for the sale of property for only £950,000. Shortly afterwards the property was put up for auction but sold beforehand for £1.2m. The applicants suspected that two of their employees had taken a bribe from the purchaser to ensure that he purchased the property cheaply with a view to a resale. After conducting inquiries, the applicants sacked the two employees and notified the Director General of Fair Trading. The director reported that no triggering event had taken place enabling him to issue a prohibition order or warning order under the 1979 Act. The applicants sought judicial review of this decision.

The High Court held that, assuming the employees had taken a bribe, a triggering event had occurred, in that they must have misrepresented the details of the purchaser's offer, contrary to the Undesirable Practices Order. The judge also held that the drafting of the Order indicates that a single event may constitute an undesirable practice.

It should be noted that the judge found that the failure to provide information as to the 'services' to be provided to the purchaser did not constitute a trigger, as the Order refers to services **ordinarily** made available. An undertaking to ensure that a particular person becomes the eventual purchaser in return for a bribe is not a service ordinarily made available.

Employer's liability, etc.

Section 3(3) of the 1979 Act provides that a person is responsible for anything done by an employee in the course of employment unless it can be shown that the employer took such steps as were reasonably practicable to prevent the employee from doing that act, or from doing in the course of his employment acts of that description.

A person is responsible for the acts of an agent. He is also responsible for anything done by a business associate unless he can show that the act was done without his connivance or consent.

Warning orders

Where a person has not complied with his statutory obligations under sections 15 and 18 to 21 of the 1979 Act (see above) or where he has engaged in an undesirable practice, the OFT may notify him that if he continues to break his obligations or engage in an undesirable practice he will be the subject of a prohibition order.

5.3 DISCRIMINATION ON THE GROUNDS OF SEX, RACE AND DISABILITY

It has been noted above that 'discrimination' is a trigger for the making of a prohibition order by the OFT under section 3 of the *Estate Agents Act* 1979. Discrimination in this sense is restricted to conduct which has given rise to a finding of discrimination or the service of a non-discrimination notice under the *Sex Discrimination Act* 1975 or the *Race Relations Act* 1976, but agents must be aware that discrimination in the limited sense of discriminating against purchasers who choose not to accept services is an undesirable practice. Discrimination in this latter sense may trigger a warning or prohibition order also.

Under the definition in Schedule 1 to the *Estate Agents Act* 1979, discrimination within section 3 means a court has made a finding of discrimination or a non-discrimination notice has been served on the agent by the Commission for Racial Equality or the Equal Opportunities Commission. Mere discrimination is not, therefore, a matter for the OFT.

Race Discrimination – Race Relations Act 1976

Section 1 of the *Race Relations Act* 1976 provides that:

> 'A person discriminates against another in any circumstances relevant for the purposes of any provision of this Act if–
>
> (a) on racial grounds he treats that other less favourably than he treats or would treat other persons; or
> (b) he applies to that other a requirement or condition which he applies or would apply equally to persons not of the same racial group as that other ...'

Furthermore, section 20(1) provides that:

> 'It is unlawful for any person concerned with the provision (for payment or not) of goods, facilities or services to the public or a section of the public to discriminate against a person who seeks to obtain or use those goods, facilities or services–
>
> (a) by refusing or deliberately omitting to provide him with any of them; or
> (b) by refusing or deliberately omitting to provide him with goods, facilities or services of the like quality, in the like manner and on the like terms as are normal in the first-mentioned person's case in relation to other members of the public or (where the person so seeking belongs to a section of the public) to other members of that section.'

The Act therefore renders unlawful any discrimination on racial grounds by an estate agent in the provision of services, whether in respect of clients or prospective purchasers and vendors.

Where, after a formal investigation, the Commission for Racial Equality (CRE) finds that there is discrimination, it may serve a non-discrimination notice. This may require a firm to change its practices and inform the CRE accordingly. Persistent discrimination may result in the CRE seeking a court injunction. It has already been seen that, under section 3 of the *Estate Agents Act* 1979, discrimination is a trigger for a warning or prohibition order by the Director General of Fair Trading.

R v Commission for Racial Equality, ex parte Cottrell and Rothon (a firm) (1989)

In this case it had been alleged that a firm of estate agents carried out a system of discrimination. One of the allegations was that non-white vendors of property had their names entered on cards which were pink, whereas white vendors had their particulars entered on white cards. Another allegation was that a non-white purchaser would not receive the same number or the same quality of properties for his consideration as a white purchaser. After a preliminary investigation, the Commission for Racial Equality (CRE) held a formal investigation and determined that the firm had contravened the Act. The firm was notified of that decision, informed that the CRE was considering issuing a non-discrimination notice, and was offered the opportunity of making oral and written representations. At the hearing of the oral representations, the witnesses on whose evidence the CRE relied upon were not present and there was no opportunity to cross-examine them. The firm sought judicial review of the conduct of the hearing.

In the Divisional Court, Lord Chief Justice Lane held that the hearing was an administrative function that did not require the formalities of cross-examination of witnesses. All that was required was that the proceedings were fair in all the circumstances. One of those circumstances was that there are no penalties in the form of fines or imprisonment – a non-discrimination notice may be served. The fact that discrimination may result in the Director General of Fair Trading taking action under the Estate Agents Act was also a circumstance, but many procedures have to be gone through before the Director General can take action. So the investigation proceedings of the CRE had been fairly conducted.

Disability Discrimination Act 1995

Section 22 of the *Disability Discrimination Act* 1995 makes it unlawful for a person with power to dispose of any premises to discriminate against a disabled person:

(a) in the terms on which he offers to dispose of those premises;
(b) by refusing to dispose of them; or
(c) in his treatment of the disabled person in relation to any list of persons in need of premises of that description.

This does not apply to a person who owns an estate or interest in the premises, and wholly occupies them unless, for the purposes of disposing of the premises, he uses the services of an estate agent.

Section 22 also makes it unlawful for a person managing any premises to discriminate against a disabled person occupying those premises:

(a) in the way he permits the disabled person to make use of any benefits or facilities;
(b) by refusing or deliberately omitting to permit the disabled person to make use of any benefits or facilities; or
(c) by evicting the disabled person, or subjecting him to any other detriment.

5.4 FLYBOARDING – TRADE DESCRIPTIONS ACT 1968

Section 13 of the *Trade Descriptions Act* 1968 states that if any person, in the course of any trade or business, gives, by whatever means, any false indication, direct or indirect, that any goods or services supplied by him are of a kind supplied to any person he shall, subject to the provisions of this Act, be guilty of an offence.

Thus it is an offence for an estate agent to erect 'Sold' boards on properties for which no instructions or authority had been received from the owners.

The question of the level of fine for this offence has been reviewed by the Court of Appeal in *R v Docklands Estates Ltd.*

R v Docklands Estates Ltd (2000)

The defendant company was charged with three offences of 'flyboarding' and elected for trial in the crown court, rather than before magistrates. The jury did not accept the defendant's claim that the boards had been erected by somebody else in order to damage the defendant's reputation, and the judge imposed a fine of £7,500 for each of the offences. This was reduced by the Court of Appeal to £2,000 for each offence. Lord Chief Justice Woolf stated that the usual £100 fine in the magistrates' courts was too low and wholly inappropriate for a commercial crime. He said that, apart from being a significant nuisance, the erection of 'fly boards' implies that a business has successfully sold the property. That can create a false impression, giving the public confidence in that company, which is not justified by its business. Furthermore, other companies that carry on their business honestly are placed at a disadvantage. The offences were committed because it was thought by the dishonest appellant estate agent that it would benefit from it and would obtain extra business. Taking account of the usual two per cent commission to be earned on the sort of properties the defendant was engaged in selling – properties in the region of £150,000 – a fine of £2,000 was appropriate.

> 'We hope that a loud and clear message will go out to magistrates' courts that the penalties that they are imposing for this class of offence are too low and should be increased to the extent that has been indicated.'

[**Note:** Estate agents should also be familiar with the conditions for deemed consent for sale boards under the *Town and Country Planning (Control of Advertisement) Regulations* 1992 (as amended).]

5.5 UNFAIR TERMS NOT INDIVIDUALLY NEGOTIATED

The *Unfair Terms in Consumer Contracts Regulations* 1999 applies to contracts between sellers or suppliers and consumers. A seller or supplier is a person acting for purposes relating to his trade, business or profession. A consumer, on the other hand, is any natural person acting outside his trade, business or profession. So an estate agency contract between a person selling his dwelling house and an estate agent would normally be a consumer contract.

The regulations provide that a contractual term which has not been individually negotiated shall be regarded as unfair if, contrary to the requirement of good faith, it causes a significant imbalance in the parties' rights and obligations arising under the contract, to the detriment of the consumer. A term is not individually negotiated where it has been drafted in advance and the consumer has therefore not been able to influence the substance of the term. An unfair term is of no effect.

The regulations do not apply to mandatory statutory provisions. Nor do they apply to the definition of the main subject matter of the contract or the remuneration or price – usually referred to as 'core terms'. However, the regulations do apply to other terms, such as those relating to notices, exemption clauses, termination and remedies. So although the commission earning event and the remuneration may be outside the regulations, other terms are regulated. If, for example, estate agents include provisions for the automatic continuation of agency agreements coupled with financial consequences for failure to terminate in accordance with a technical procedure, this could be regarded as unfair.

The regulations also provide that any term (including a core term) in a written contract must be expressed in plain, intelligible language. In the case of ambiguity, the interpretation most favourable to the consumer will prevail.

There are provisions authorising the Office of Fair Trading and other bodies to obtain an injunction against a person or body using unfair terms.

Price escalation clauses

A provision for the payment of a higher price or commission in certain circumstances, such as late payment, may fall within the regulations. If such a sum is not a genuine term as to price it may be unfair.

Bairstow Eves London Central Ltd v Smith (2004)

The parties had entered an estate agency agreement under which the so-called 'standard commission rate' was three per cent plus VAT. However, there was also an 'early payment discounted commission rate' of 1.5 per cent plus VAT. This rate applied if payment in full was made within ten working days of completion of the sale. The vendors instructed their solicitors to pay the agent's fee out of the completion monies, but the solicitors inexcusably failed to pay the full amount and there was a shortfall of £387 out of a total bill approaching £3,000. The £387 remained unpaid and so the claimant agents eventually claimed commission at the three per cent rate less what had already been paid. By the time of the court hearing, the £387 had been paid. The county court judge found the provision for the three per cent rate to be an unfair term under the regulations.

The issue for the High Court on appeal was whether the 'standard commission rate' was, in reality, a default provision, or whether it was the real commission rate with the vendors having an option to pay the lower amount. If the latter, it would be a term as to price and so beyond the scope of the regulations. On the evidence of the negotiations and the fact that the claimant would have been unlikely to obtain business at three per cent, the High Court held that it was a default provision. Therefore the regulations applied and so the finding of the county court judge that it was an unfair term was upheld. He had described the provision as a trap for consumers as it could operate where there was simply a misunderstanding between them and their solicitors, as in the case itself. It was, he had said, 'not a good standard of commercial morality or practice'.

Technical requirements for termination of agency contract

Some agency contracts require certain formalities to be observed by the client if he wishes to terminate the agency contract. For example, termination by letter sent by recorded delivery. The indicative (and non-exhaustive) list of unfair terms in Schedule 2 of the Regulations includes the following:

> 'automatically extending a contract of fixed duration where the consumer does not indicate otherwise, when the deadline fixed for the consumer to express his desire not to extend the contract is unreasonably early'.

Although this is obviously not the same as the standard fixed-term sole agency contract which is automatically continued unless the client gives notice, it indicates that artificial attempts to restrict the right of termination may be regarded as unfair. Therefore mandatory notice requirements, such as the requirement of recorded delivery, could be at risk. The client may have genuinely attempted to terminate by ordinary post, but the contract would still be operative. Similarly, a requirement to give a long period of notice may be regarded as unfair.

Christie Owen & Davies plc v King (1998)

The parties entered into a sole selling rights agreement for a minimum period of six months. The agreement could be terminated by four weeks' written notice, otherwise it would continue indefinitely. If it was terminated prematurely, i.e. during the six-month period, remuneration was due.

The contract provided that notice 'must be served by recorded delivery ...'. After nine months, the client telephoned the agents to enquire about progress and was informed that the person dealing with the property had been transferred to the London office. He therefore told the agents he was taking the property off the market and sent a letter on the following day, by ordinary post, confirming this.

One of the matters in issue was whether the contract had been validly terminated. Counsel for the client conceded that the requirement of recorded delivery was mandatory. However, he contended that on the wording of the clauses the requirement only applied to notice of premature termination, not termination after six months. (The clauses were not without ambiguity.) The Court seems to have preferred the view of counsel for the agent that the requirement of recorded delivery applied to any notice. However, this matter did not have to be determined as the agents won on another ground (above, 4.5.1) and the *Unfair Terms in Consumer Contracts Regulations* were not in issue.

Even though the *Unfair Terms in Consumer Contracts Regulations* were not in issue, the concession by counsel for the client that the notice requirements were mandatory may be a little surprising. However, the application of the regulations in future cases will necessitate the judicial examination of such clauses, so it is doubtful that this is the last word on recorded delivery requirements.

5.6 ACCOMMODATION AGENCIES ACT 1953

The *Accommodation Agencies Act* 1953 makes it a criminal offence for a person to take payment from a prospective tenant for supplying addresses or for registering his requirements. (An agent can, of course, earn commission from the landlord for finding a tenant.) It is also an offence to issue an advertisement, list or other document describing any house as being to let without the authority of the owner of the house or his agent. Obviously the agent cannot claim commission for an illegal act.

Even if the agent provides a list of addresses in return for a payment which is returned if no accommodation is found, there is still an offence under the terms of section 1 of the Act.

McInnes v Clarke (1955)

Any tenant seeking accommodation from the appellant agent would be asked what rent he was willing to pay. He would then be told that the agent's commission for finding accommodation would be equal to one week's rent, and that half was payable now, as a deposit, and the other half due when accommodation was found. He would then be supplied with a list of addresses. In the event of no accommodation being found, the deposit was returned in full. The agent claimed that he was not in breach of the *Accommodation Agencies Act* 1953 because, looked at as a whole, he received commission only for finding accommodation, and received nothing if he provided a list of addresses which turned out to be useless. The divisional court held that, as it was the case that no list would be provided unless the deposit was paid, the agent had accepted payment in consideration of supplying addresses. The fact that the deposit was returned was not material.

The Act does not make it unlawful for an agent to charge commission to a tenant for finding accommodation which he actually takes. So the fact that the agent also supplies addresses is not an offence, as no payment is made for them.

Saunders v Soper (1975)

In this case the agent charged the equivalent of one week's rent in the event (a) of the agent finding acceptable accommodation and (b) of the client actually becoming the tenant of such accommodation. The agent would provide an address or addresses for the client to view, but no money would change hands unless the client obtained accommodation. The House of Lords held that the transaction was lawful, as the consideration was for finding accommodation, not for supplying addresses. The case of *McInnes v Clarke* was distinguished.

5.7 RENT ACT 1977 – PROHIBITION OF PREMIUMS

Section 119 of the *Rent Act 1977* provides that any person who, as a condition of the grant, renewal or continuance of a protected tenancy, requires, in addition to the rent, the payment of any premium or the making of any loan shall be guilty of an offence.

Section 120 imposes a similar prohibition on the payment to any person of any premium or loan as a condition of the assignment of a protected tenancy.

The phrase 'any person' has been held to be wide enough to include landlords, tenants, agents or middlemen (*Farrell v Alexander*).

(As to the authority of an agent to accept an illegal premium, this is dealt within *Navarro v Moregrand Ltd* and *Saleh v Robinson* at 1.1.6 above. As to the criminal liability of the principal for the acceptance by the agent of an illegal premium, this is covered in *Barker v Levinson*, ibid.)

5.8 RESTRICTIVE PRACTICES

Where a partner or employee covenants not to practice for a certain time within a certain distance on termination of the partnership or employment, the court will only enforce such a restrictive covenant if the claimant establishes that:

(a) he has a legitimate interest capable of being protected, such as the goodwill of an estate agency business;
(b) the covenant is no more than 'adequate' to protect the interest – in other words it is not excessive in time, duration or prohibited activities;
(c) without the enforcement of the covenant the interest or goodwill could be injured or damaged.

The reason for the rule is that it is a general principle of the common law that a person can exercise any lawful trade or calling wherever he wishes. The law frowns upon any interference with trade and, for reasons of public policy, will not enforce an agreement which merely protects the claimant against competition. (Article 81 of the EC Treaty also places limits on restrictive trade practices.)

Espley v Williams (1997)

The plaintiff and defendant entered into a partnership to run an estate agency in Christchurch. By the partnership agreement, the defendant covenanted that he would not, within a period of two years from the date of termination of the partnership, practice as an estate agent, either on his own account or in conjunction with anybody else, within two miles of the premises. The defendant left the partnership in May 1995 and later that year obtained employment with a rival estate agent within a two-mile radius. The plaintiff sought an injunction.

The defendant contended that another two-year covenant he had agreed to – not to solicit business or otherwise interfere with the relationship between the plaintiff and any former customers – was sufficient to protect the plaintiff's goodwill. He claimed that the two-mile covenant merely protected the plaintiff from legitimate competition.

The judge found that the two-mile covenant was not a mere covenant against competition but protected the goodwill of the business. The defendant's intimate knowledge of the residential market in Christchurch coupled with experience could give a competitive edge to a rival. Recommendations to third parties to instruct the defendant based on past dealings could also damage the plaintiff, and in that instance the defendant would not have solicited or canvassed those instructions.

The Court of Appeal found no reason to fault the judge's findings, so the defendant's appeal was dismissed. Lord Justice Henry observed that a non-solicitation covenant is difficult, if not impossible, to enforce in practice, and the judge was entitled to find that it did not protect the plaintiff's interest. As regards the time and distance of the restriction, Lord Justice Henry observed that it was customary in Christchurch and had, unsurprisingly, not been attacked by the defendant. However, he noted that the mere fact that a restriction is customary does not tie the judge's hands.

Index

The Case in Point Series

The *Case in Point* series is an exciting new set of concise practical guides to legal issues in land, property and construction. Written for the property professional, they get straight to the key issues in a refreshingly jargon-free style.

Areas covered:
Negligence in Valuation and Surveys
Stock Code: 6388
Published: December 2002

Party Walls
Stock Code: 7269
Published: May 2004

Service Charges
Stock Code: 7272
Published: June 2004

Rights of Lights
Due for publication: December 2004

Lease Renewal
Due for publication: January 2005

Rent Review
Due for publication: January 2005

Construction Adjudication
Due for publication: February 2005

If you would like to be kept informed when new *Case in Point* titles are published, please e-mail rbmarketing@rics.org.uk

How to order:
All RICS Books titles can be ordered direct by:
☎ Telephoning 0870 333 1600 (Option 3)
🖱 Online at www.ricsbooks.com
🖷 E-mail mailorder@rics.org.uk